PLEASE...

LET ME SEE MY SON

by

Thomas Moore

**Grosvenor House
Publishing Limited**

The right of Thomas Moore to be identified as the author of this
work has been asserted by him in accordance with Section 78
of the Copyright, Designs and Patents Act 1988

The book cover picture is copyright to Thomas Moore

This book is published by
Grosvenor House Publishing Ltd
28-30 High Street, Guildford, Surrey, GU1 3EL.
www.grosvenorhousepublishing.co.uk

A CIP record for this book
is available from the British Library

ISBN 978-1-78148-616-0

The story of a father's fight against parental alienation, the loophole in UK Family Law, and the apathy of the system we entrust with a duty of care to our children.

A story of our time, of what is happening to fathers (and some mothers) and their children up and down this land.

Contents

Foreword
By Karen Woodall

This book is a story of our time. It is the story of divorce, separation and the way fathers are faced with almost insurmountable barriers to having ongoing relationships with their children when the parents separate. In many ways this is every father's story. But it is also a story that will resonate with some mothers who, like Thomas in this book, also face being eradicated from their children's lives.

This book is published during the year that the coalition government is proposing to change the Children Act 1989. This is widely touted by some fathers' groups as being the change in the law that will stop fathers from experiencing what Thomas went through. Unfortunately, as some judges have already made clear, it is unlikely to change very much at all and so, whilst the government appears to be creating change, the experience on the ground for dads is likely to continue to be similar to the story – the one contained in this book.

When I first began to work with separated fathers I too believed the rhetoric of the academics who work in this field. These academics are overwhelmingly women and most of them study their subject using a feminist perspective. The influence that these women have on the experience of dads like Thomas should not be underestimated. Whilst they may be sitting in the hallowed halls of some of our most prestigious universities, their reach into family life is powerful and enduring. The studies that are churned out are mostly about the way in which fathers are not good enough, not interested enough or not safe enough. The perspective of these academics is that women and children should be able to leave a relationship unhindered by the desires of fathers to continue to have relationships with their children. To underscore that point, study after study has been produced to show how fathers are not necessary, not important in children's lives and their absence does not have an impact. In reading about family separation through the eyes of the academics, you would be forgiven for believing that the only thing that fathers can do after separation that matters is pay their child maintenance.

Thankfully, however, there are some studies that demonstrate that children need their fathers after separation and some academics understand that dads have more to give than money. Judy Dunn, from the Institute of Psychiatry[1], has done a huge amount of work in studying the impact of separation on children and her findings are unequivocal. Children who do best after separation are those with a strong relationship with their father. For those of us who work with separated families, this research bears out our reality and gives voice to the truth, which has been long repressed.

---

[1] Dunn et al: Children and Their Changing Families: Routledge 2008

I have worked with separating families for over two decades. For some of that time I worked to support mothers and their children. As I did so I began to realise that whilst we were supporting these 'lone' parents, we were assuming that the fathers were entirely absent. When we began to ask mothers about their children's relationships with their fathers, we were therefore astounded to find that almost all of the children we were seeing had some kind of relationship with their father. These 'lone' parents, who were portrayed as being 'abandoned' by the fathers of their children by the media, by government and, ultimately, by our services, were far from that. That was the point at which we decided to support not just mums but dads as well and to build a service to families that would assist them to rebuild a co-operative relationship after separation – something that all of the international studies show as hugely beneficial to children.

Looking back now, it seems somewhat naïve to think that we could open our doors to mums and dads and solve their difficulties just by working in a different way. Some thirteen years on from that decision and the ways in which fathers are disadvantaged after separation are just as present, just as powerful. Though we work with the whole family now, it is more often fathers who come through our doors in despair and dads who tell us over and over again that their relationship with their children is being blocked.

Thomas was one of those dads. Shut out and silenced for such a long time, he walked through the door at the Centre for Separated Families and immediately started to talk. I made tea and listened; I could tell that he had suffered enormously.

There is a common misperception about family separation, that only those parents who are in high conflict situations go into the court system. In fact, many parents find themselves in the court system simply because the other parent will not enter into any kind of communication with them. In these situations it is less of a high conflict problem that drives a parent to court and more of a last resort. The very conflicted parents are often those who have had to go into the court system because nothing else they have done has worked. Fathers (more often than mothers) find themselves being blamed for conflict that was only caused by the refusal of the other parent to engage in communicate in the first place.

Thomas, like many other dads before him, told me about his relationship with his son and as he did so I was able to take a better look at this man. He looked tired and frustrated and extremely sad, especially as he talked about his son and the length of time that he had tried, without success, to get to see him.

Thomas's story was a familiar one and as he continued to talk I made notes and scribbled down the questions that I would want to ask his son's other parent. I didn't know then that I would never get to put those questions directly to her.

After our session I invited Thomas to take part in a course that we were running called Children in Focus. This course was focused upon helping parents to work out their differences and improve their ability to parent together. Thomas, in what I would come to know as his own, inimitable style, said "What the hell, I'll give it a go,". And give it a go he did, all sixty-plus hours of it.

In my work it is important that I get to know parents as much as possible. I also meet and work with children, at least once and sometimes on a regular basis. These days I specialise in working with cases where children resist or refuse to see a parent. But back then, although I had read about parental alienation, I had not worked with families where it had occurred.

Thomas's case, therefore, was one of the first of its kind that I had worked on, and what an introduction. This case remains the most severe case of alienation I have worked with and one that has taught me a huge amount about the phenomenon as it plays out in real lives.

Cases where parents are deliberately preventing a child from having a relationship with a parent are not unusual in the UK. Legislation in this country makes it very difficult for fathers (sometimes mothers too, but most often fathers) to maintain their parenting role if the other parent is determined to stop it. In most cases, however, when someone is brought in from the outside, the parent who is what is termed "implacably hostile" will soften and try at least to give a good impression. Not in this case.

Jane's determination to prevent Thomas from seeing his son went as far as making allegations against anyone who worked with Thomas and it was soon clear that I was in that category in her mind. As I was prevented again and again from being able to meet their son, I started to wonder what else might be going on. It is not often that parents will remain so implacably hostile and so determined to stop a relationship that they will act in the way that Jane had been acting. Alarm bells were ringing faintly somewhere.

In many of these cases, where children refuse to see a parent, the assumption by professionals is that this is because of something that a parent has done. This was no exception. In CAFCASS report after CAFCASS report, I could see the finger of blame pointing at Thomas; even when it was not pointing directly at him, there were inferences, suggestions that if he just changed his parenting style a bit, was a bit less boisterous perhaps, things might change. In one, frankly offensive, report, a CAFCASS officer appeared to be almost goading him about his lack of time with his son, asking him questions about whether he paid child maintenance and making references to being angry. I could see, as I pieced the whole thing together, what Thomas had been through and that he had shouldered not only the blame for his son refusing to see him but the responsibility for coping with it all of these years. As I read, I wondered how he had managed.

The alarm bells that had been ringing faintly somewhere started to jangle urgently as I read further through the paperwork on this case, particularly when I got to the school reports and the nurses' reports. Thomas had told me on several occasions that he could predict when his son would be absent from school and had provided me with a calendar of his contacts that had been cancelled. Now, as I sat, matching school absences to missed contacts, GP visits to planned holidays with dad and illnesses that had little or no explanation, I could see that what Thomas had been telling me all of these months was, in fact, true. There was a pattern to David's illnesses and absences and they did match the contact times and holidays. I put on another hat – my *what if* hat – and went through the evidence again, this time asking myself the question "What if there is something wrong with Jane that is being projected onto David, something that she doesn't want Thomas to know about, something that would cause her to cancel and break contact after contact after contact arrangement?"

It was that *what if* hat that allowed me to keep on supporting Thomas. It allows me to think the unthinkable, something that not many family court professionals seem capable of. Working through the paperwork again, I called Thomas and asked him to come and see me. When he and his wife Annie arrived that day, we began the forensic work of piecing together the possibilities. That day was the first of my years of forensic work with families affected by parental alienation and it shifted my thinking forever on the deeper, unseen problems that face children when families separate.

The story that you are about to read is a real story of our time. It is, on the face of it, an unusual story, not least because of the reality of what was happening in the family system and how we came to uncover that. It is, at the same time, an everyday story, it is a story of what is happening to fathers (and some mothers) and their children up and down this land. It is the story of a father's enduring love for his child and his instinctive awareness that something was wrong. It is about determination and bravery and finally about family and the ties that we bind around each other to provide either safety, love and protection, or the opposite.

I keep in touch with Thomas and Annie and, whilst I never did get to meet David, I feel that I know him. In every alienated child I work with I remember David and each and every time I meet a parent who is alienated I remember Thomas. Each time I tell a dad to sit on his hands in the courtroom (a tactic I used with Thomas to stop him from becoming over emotional), I am right back there, in that courtroom, with him. Fast forward to the present day and I hear from Thomas of the ongoing journey that has unfolded since the judge that day finally grasped the fact that something was terribly wrong. That journey continues to inform my work and helps me to understand what else I can do, after the court process, that brings better outcomes for children.

In so many ways this case changed my working life and led me to begin the process of building services to support families where parental alienation occurs. I am grateful to Thomas and Annie for allowing me to support them through their journey and learn from them what it means to survive and thrive, as a family.

I am amazed at their resilience, courage and tenacity.

I guarantee that you will be, too.

Introduction

It was on the morning of February 22, 2007, when my son was all but lost to me, that I saw the headlines in the news: politicians and social leaders would attend a summit on the recent spate of gun crimes in London. The story referred to three teenagers being shot dead and explained that then-opposition leader David Cameron would appear on *BBC Breakfast* quoting the need for long-term social change. Cameron emphasised particularly the need for fathers to stand by their children: he suggested a change to the tax structure to give married couples an increased tax allowance and to further pursue fathers who fail to support their children financially.

"Here we go, just what I need to start my day," I said to myself. "Another burst of bullshit from a politician keen to arouse public anger and make an impact at the ballot box." As a true Englishman, I made myself a cup of tea, muttered derogatory remarks about the news story, and turned my attention instead to that day's Sudoku.

Even focused on the cryptic puzzle before me, I couldn't waste the adrenaline rush from the news subject and decided to email David Cameron, to an address located through chance by hitting my computer's keyboard out of frustration in a manner comparable to that of an orang-utan finding the zookeeper swinging in his tyre.

Dear Mr Cameron,
What of the benefit system that serves to encourage parenthood as an alternative to a career? A benefit system that serves to undermine the father's role. What of a legal system that fails to protect children from emotional abuse? A hypocrisy that quotes 'the needs of the child are foremost' yet is powerless to ensure a child grows up knowing the love of their entire family? I dare you David Cameron, raise these issues. If you truly wish fathers to have more input into the lives of their children you might begin by addressing what stops a vast number from doing so. Correct this and our children's lives will be enhanced, as will our society, and there may even be an economic benefit to the country for you politicians to lay claim to!

I did not harbour any illusion that I would receive a reply, and no response ever arrived. Possibly his server crashed or his spam filter intercepted the message, or maybe he did read it, muttered a few derogatory remarks of his own and thought, "Here we go, just what I need to start my day."

By the time a man reaches the respectable age of forty-four, there is a fair assumption that his parents will have shed the concern of his announcement that he is about to have a child with his girlfriend, but such was the situation I found myself in. It was a cold December day in the run-up to Christmas when my girlfriend – who will be referred to as Jane and who was a few months' shy of turning forty and fewer months' shy of giving birth to her first child – and I were sat in my parents' living room.

"Well, Mum", I began, and my mother burst out laughing before I could finish my sentence. She was both delighted and amused, and my father shook his head while wearing a broad smile that served to override the shake of the head. My brother had already made them great grandparents and this was not my first venture into parenthood – I had a fourteen-year-old daughter from a relationship that ended eight years prior to our sitting in the living room breaking the news of another addition to the family.

First foray into parenthood or not, I knew that, having been in this particular relationship for barely more than two years, things were about to change forever. What I didn't know, however, was how much pain and heartache I was about to unleash onto my unsuspecting family.

According to the testimony of friends, I was the victim of a setup from day one. When I look at the demands, lies and skilful half-truths with hindsight, I can't help but agree. When I first started the relationship with Jane, the woman that became my son's mother, I received a call from an old friend of mine that also knew my new acquaintance, and warned me that she was on a schedule – she wanted children by a certain time. At this point in my life, I had been single for a number of years and made a point of discussing the issue of children with Jane. She informed me in no unclear terms that she had no desire to be a parent herself and confirmed this to be true, in my mind at least, by relaying a deeply emotional story of having had an abortion roughly six months prior to our meeting.

As a careful person, I treated my relation with this woman in the same way I had with any other woman who came into my life: I had taken precautions and even noted dates, making sure I knew where in the month we were. This time around, however, I was outmanoeuvred.

I spotted the early signs of pregnancy first, while she denied it could be true and refused to visit a doctor to confirm one way or the other. It was another ten days before she finally revealed that she also thought she may be pregnant, and another week before a doctor confirmed it. With neither of us supposedly wanting children we openly discussed the option of a termination, and we booked an ultrasound scan to date the pregnancy in order to decide what options we really had.

The nurse on duty was known to us both and openly asked if we were there to "determine the timing for a possible termination". Jane replied in the affirmative while I remained silent. The scan showed an advanced pregnancy and we returned home to plan parenthood.

Later, in a statement to the court, Jane was quoted as saying that she "never contemplated a termination". If such a statement was true then she was guilty of entrapment. I was also falsely accused of saying that I did not want "him" (the "him" being my son, David) in a deliberate misrepresentation of fact. What I had actually said, a year prior, was that I did not want a child 'with Jane' – but once David arrived in 1999 how could I hesitate to love him?

CHAPTER 1

My first court hearing for the second round of legal bouts took place six years after the pregnancy, in 2005. That it occurred on the longest day of the year on June 21 proved to be something of an omen for the long and relentless road ahead. Not only was it the longest day, it was also one of the hottest, and while the others in the waiting room were suitably attired I was sweating for England in formal dress. To add to my discomfort, I was fifty minutes early so would be basking in the heat for some time. I asked the usher if the air-conditioning could be switched on. With a smile, he pointed to the single half-open pane in a wall of south-facing glass and replied, "It is on."

They call it Family Court, and I am sure that identical stories are repeated day in and day out, like a real-life *Groundhog Day*. Before me were two other fathers, and from what they were being told by their legal represent-atives I figured that they were being inaugurated into the legal system in a last-ditch attempt to be granted access to their children. In a system that almost universally favours the maternal over the paternal, a father seeking to be granted access to their child can be a frustrating and lonely uphill battle.

Those talking lowered their voices, but in a small clinical room of seventies design little sound is actually suppressed, and I heard identical vocabulary being told to each father as I was told four years prior when I first filed court papers to see my son. Although the entirety of the conversation eluded my ears, I heard keywords, like "half hour", "supervised", "once a week", "violence" and "abusive": enough to paint a clear enough picture of what they were being told. The face of one father displayed extreme frustration while the other lowered his head in sadness. Compassion swept through me and I had an urge to walk over and talk to the men, both of whom looked as though they had reverted to a state of boyhood. I wanted to try to ease their emotions by reminding them that the system is senseless, that there are delaying strategies open to the mothers and their legal representation may be interpreted as eager to keep the bills mounting so their bank balance blossomed like a garden in late spring. More than anything, though, I wanted to shout so loudly that those on the street outside might hear the words: "It is all futile!"

One fundamental difference between Family Law and Criminal Law is that within the former, you are not innocent until proven guilty; instead, you are open to any accusation the resident parent wishes to suggest and pursue, regardless of how absurd it is – worse still, character references or track records are not taken into consideration, not even any past history the accuser has of making false allegations. While being ostracised from your child, you are still expected to pay child support, and the Child Support Agency (CSA) can demand any figure it wants; should you refrain from paying and are taken to court, there is no recourse but to pay. As the non-resident parent you are expected to maintain your employment, pay taxes and child support, while also paying your own legal fees, taking time off work to attend court and related meetings, and simultaneously focus on your work to keep your employer happy. Conversely, the non-working resident parent will qualify for seemingly endless Legal Aid. To me, all this begs two questions: "What chance does a regular respectable working non-resident parent have?" and, "Where is the justice for our children?"

I looked at the fathers across from me again. I wanted to tell them, "The only thing this system guarantees is a bill, and a bloody big one, financially and emotionally. Stop now!" I refrained, of course; such words would have helped no one, including my own case, and I couldn't bring myself to be so cruel as to extinguish the last glimmer of hope that these fathers may be helped by the British legal system. Besides, judging from their outward expressions, it seemed they knew this just as much as I did. Certainly the usher did, and it appeared as though the emotional aspect of the job did not affect him. He was pleasantly efficient but no emotion was to be seen, which, I suspect, would happen to anyone should they bear witness to the same scenes week after week. The usher's job is more than shuffling papers and herding the public: he is the witness that is never called upon to testify; he sees, but cannot comment on, the bitterness and cruelty of some parents that are so blinded in their rage and personal issues that they use and abuse the innocent children that they insist they love but invariably employ as pawns in their scramble for the moral high ground. What man wouldn't shut down some emotions to this drama after seeing it enough times?

This was my second bout of legal proceedings to gain access to my son, and I had been where the two fathers opposite me were: naïvely placing all my faith in justice, trusting that each child has a basic human right of having access to both of its parents. At the time, my motto was "Common sense will prevail", although it later, as my faith began to waver, changed to "Surely common sense will prevail", then "Common sense will eventually prevail". Immeasurable variations followed until I eventually reached the conclusion that common sense can only actually prevail when everyone is prepared to be rational, and in such a setting as a court, where everyone wants what they feel is owed to them, rationality seldom appears. Nonetheless, employing hindsight once again, I do not look back and think I would have changed my course of action; as much of a waste of time as it seemed to be, not trying every legal means available can be used as further ammunition against you.

Being denied access to a child is an extremely difficult and heart-wrenching experience, and people deal with it in different ways. Some are unable to control their frustration and others simply walk away in the hope of causing no further stress or confusion to the child. I have complete sympathy and understanding to all of these parents, but I could not give up and lose access to my son. I had by this point been through a long and painful battle, but I was still learning simple facts. For example, when you are in court defending yourself against allegations – even if they are completely untrue – you are judged as disreputable to the extent that you are accused, on the presupposition that both parties before the judge wish to discredit each other. Any attempts to express what you believe to be "in the best interest of the child" will be distorted and considered retaliation, rather than an objective statement. Essentially, it is important to accept that you are damned no matter how you go about it, and despair can cause you to think that there is no right way to conduct yourself. It appears sometimes that the legal system fails to recognise that, for things to have degenerated into necessitating multiple trips to court, there is little chance of reconciling differences. If the parent with care so chooses, the wheels are in motion for the non-resident parent to be slowly alienated. In my early years I genuinely believed that our only chance is to let those judging us see us turn the other cheek, but I was proven to be naïvely optimistic. This biblical example is flawed because it requires those in a position of power to witness the act but the people who you work with either fail to recognise or record such an action.

A few years prior to this particular round in court, when my son was not yet two years old, I was successfully issued a court order for access after an expensive and extensive process. On the day I turned up at Jane's to collect him, I was told he was unavailable. Despite knowing it would do no good, I reminded Jane and her visiting parents of the court order and the punishments for being held in contempt. The door was closed, with me on the outside of it. I became angry, as I believe many others would have been, and looking back I can see that was the plan all along from Jane. I have never been violent, but displaying anger presents a perfect opportunity for the accusation that the emotion cannot be controlled, which is a damning statement in court. Short of kicking the door down or screaming through the window to let me see my son, which truly would have ended any chance I may have had of gaining access, I had no choice but to return to court. In the time immediate after being refused entry, I peacefully displayed my disappointment by sitting on their garden wall, considering waiting for the morning to pass me by. I didn't though; the wall was cold and damp and after fifteen minutes my bones reminded me it wasn't a good idea to be sitting there, so I drove home.

Thirty minutes after getting home a local police officer arrived at my property apparently Jane had called them to report my brief sit on the wall. It turned out to be one of those occasions where small towns have their advantages, because this particular officer was an old neighbour and I invited him inside. Still, old neighbour or not, a visit from the police is rarely a courtesy call, and it was a curious fact that he was in my property despite me having a court order and not doing anything wrong. He was an affable man though, and I delighted in telling him not only of my situation, but also that the mother of my son privately claimed the local chief constable had assaulted her and suggested he not be left alone in her company, lest she could hinder his chances of promotion.

When the police officer left, I was alone to express my frustrations inside my home. I had done nothing wrong and had a visit from the police; despite the contempt of the court order the police were powerless to do anything. When I returned to court the first thing mentioned was how the police had to visit me. The judge frowned and said nothing other than a warning that the order must be adhered to. Somehow, I was portrayed to be the bad person and my son had yet another extension of how long he would not be seeing his father. The paradox was starting to become clear to me: I was damned regardless of what I did, and our son was the loser on each occasion.

Several years into the court battles, with David a few days shy of turning six, I was still struggling for access. I had clung to the court order for a couple of years, though sadly my work meant that I was only seeing my son about half as often as I could. My job meant I spent much time abroad, often six weeks away and four weeks in England. To accommodate time with my son, wherever possible I tried to make my trips occur on a Monday and only last twelve days, but the upshot of that was a drastic increase in the cost of airline tickets. To make it worse, when I missed a week, my son would then be away for a week, and so the cycle went. If my vocation meant my being away for two weeks then I could expect to go a month without seeing my son; somehow, despite Jane's stretched finances, he was on holiday an average of six times a year. Added to this were the numerous cancelled visits due to illness, or the Sunday parties Jane insisted he attend with her. The time we were supposed to spend together was methodically eroded in such a manner that it was not a breach of the court order, and I could do nothing about it or talk with Jane because she refused to communicate with me or agree to mediation with a third party. Despite the years that had passed, we had made no real progress and she had vowed to move "a long, long way away" if I were to secure an overnight order. On one occasion she even questioned me: "Why do you want a small boy to stay overnight with you?" in a tone and manner that suggested I was a pervert. I was caught between a rock and a hard place. There was one occasion where my son made a seemingly miraculous recovery from a three-week illness, during which time he had missed both school and contact time with me. I was unsurprised to hear of his recovery because that afternoon he and his mother were due to go on holiday. I knew at this point that once again I would have to readdress the situation. Years had gone by and I could no longer tolerate the excuses of missed time or the callous treatment of my son, so I went to the courts and filed papers again, but this time I did so alone, without any legal representative or the extortionate fees that accompany them.

I had actually collected the forms a year prior to this, following another period of frustrated contact. I had at that point discovered a helpline on the Internet and I sent an email detailing my situation, to which I received a prompt and courteous reply with advice on diplomatic and legal possibilities. I took immediate comfort in receiving feedback from a source that did not know me from Adam but which was informed of the system's boundaries and cared enough to inform me of them. Despite the years that had unfolded, I was still naïve enough to decide to ignore the advice and work under the assumption that things would mellow if I said nothing and did not rock the boat.

When the separation first took place and after failed mediation sessions I tried what I regarded as a 'common sense' approach with Jane. We had a meeting, overseen by her parents, in which I acknowledged that there would be large sums of money involved with legal action and instead suggested that I invest a lump sum into a tax efficient bond for our son's future, and agreed to maintain the voluntary child support that I had been paying since Jane left. This suggestion was immediately dismissed as blackmail, and I was offered visitation of thirty minutes once a week, which would be supervised by either Jane or her father. Consequently, rather than put the money into a bond for my son, I used it to pay for the first legal battle. Within eighteen months, I had spent that money and a further fifty per cent thanks to a solicitor who consistently had the aroma of tobacco and whisky regardless of the hour and who insisted on three trips to the Magistrates Court before seeing the need to progress to Family Court, plus there were interviews with the Children and Family Court Advisory and Support Service (CAFCASS) too numerous to count and seven appearances in court. When I presented this latest set of forms to the court, I was informed that they were now outdated and I would be required to complete the latest versions – which, I was told, now cost fifty per cent more than those I had completed.

I was of course aware of the inherent dangers of stirring the pot of bitterness that surfaced during the previous court liaisons, but the system's operation meant I had no choice but to go through the process once again. I suppose that the rules' creators thought that the act of serving the papers would deter additional frustration, that a respondent would know that further aggravation of an existing court order would be detrimental to them in a future hearing. If that is what they thought, they were as wrong as it is possible to be, because here I was, on the longest day of the year, wiping sweat from my brow. It was two months since I had last seen my son.

As I stood with my back to the entrance I heard voices and recognised them as belonging to Jane and her seemingly omnipresent father. So usual was the sight of him shadowing her that I dubbed him Kevin Costner, an eighty-four-year-old version of the *Bodyguard*. Initially, I thought he was a doting father blindly believing his daughter's version of events, but as the years – and access struggles – continued, I came to realise that he was no better than his offspring, and perhaps the root cause. On the very first unsupervised contact I had with my son I saw him hiding behind a tree over the road from my home, spying on us. I ran outside with my camera and photographed him; while my plan had been to shout at him to leave us alone, the image of seeing a man attempting to hide behind a tree less than a third his girth was too much and I burst out laughing. On a second occasion I returned home to find him reading through my mail, after pressuring my neighbour into letting him into the house. I couldn't blame the neighbour, she was one of the world's genuine sweet old ladies who had been my building companion for a decade, and I had entrusted her with an emergency key for my door. The only positive was that I was able to mention these incidents during my interviews with CAFCASS, and I hoped they would help my character portrayal – after all, if I was a violent man I would have hit him rather than take his photograph, or challenged him as he rifled through my personal mail. Alas, no such considerations were taken aboard.

As names were given to the usher I noticed a well-groomed male attired in a generic suit and matching tie rise from his seat and greet Jane and her father. This solicitor exchanged muted words with them and then came over to me. We exchanged a sweaty handshake and I deduced from his limp grip and the split-second eye contact that he had no emotional involvement here, it was just another day at the office.

"I understand you want overnight contact with your son," he said, and when I replied in the affirmative he informed me that Jane said our child was "not ready for overnight and I suggest that we therefore request the court to conduct a CAFCASS report."

I drew a long breath and tried to make eye contact before informing him that Jane had maintained my son was not ready for overnight visits for four years, and that I wanted to give the facts to the judge and allow him to have the final say on the necessity of a report. I knew a report would mean more delays, but I could see no other choice. The solicitor nodded and walked back to Jane's side of the room.

The bell rang, the judge was ready, and in this return bout of legal hearings, round one had officially started.

CHAPTER 2

I was by now familiar with the walk to the hearing room as I had done it multiple times before. Each time I did so, my mind raced with similar thoughts surfing the waves of adrenaline. In the same manner as watching a flick-book reel, I saw rapid flashes of every insane issue that I was being put through as a result of the legal process. I noticed an irony in the fact that a century ago children were put to work in coalmines and chimneys, and in a bid to protect them from harm parents must now jump through numerous legal hoops just to be able to see them. I was not in the court out of respect of the legal system; I was there because I had no alternative.

Jane and I both sat before the judge, with her in contempt of a court order and myself in silent disrespect of the system. I understood that, as I had been the one to serve the papers, I would be the first of us to speak. Yet when the judge addressed us, it was Jane's solicitor who spoke first. I cannot say I was surprised, but I was frustrated; I wanted to interrupt with the question, "Whose shilling is this?" but I managed to bite my tongue. While I refrained from doing so, I have no doubts that my frustration of being cast aside combined with all the stress from events leading up to that moment showed on my face, so perhaps my emotions were registered. Whether they were or not, I knew in that moment that I was there only to gain access to my son, and I would gain nothing – and possibly lose everything – by arguing over court etiquette.

I got my chance to speak shortly after anyway, when the judge enquired of me why I was applying to the court. I interpreted this question to mean one of two things: he was either mistakenly trying to set a casual atmosphere in the court, or he was tacitly admitting that he had not read my application, which was at that moment residing in his left hand. I spoke neither of these thoughts to him, but decided I couldn't let the matter go completely unmentioned. I apologised and expressed my embarrassment at having no alternative but to be back in court – this was mostly true, but I also felt that if I had rights without going to court I would not have returned there. I pointed briefly to the application in his hand and continued with carefully spoken words that I think concealed all of my contempt: "Sir, as I have stated in the C1 form, I have three concerns: the lack of contact happening under the existing court order; the lack of progress during the past four years to move toward weekend contact; and our son's behaviour."

The judge responded by asking me to provide more details on the lack of contact. I could quite easily have recited the facts off the top of my head, and probably while riding a unicycle and juggling swords, but in emulation of the solicitors' tactics to appear more credible I instead read from my notes. When I had finished, the judge agreed that contact to that moment had not been acceptable, and then rambled for a while about communication between parents. I had heard an almost identical lecture four years prior to this one, and that time I openly addressed the court: "If anyone here can tell me of one thing I have been granted with regard to my son, without having had to come to court to get it, I will listen to them lecture me on communicating with this woman." No one had responded, and the judge was well aware of the failed mediation, the extensive lengths to which I had been to try to see my son. At this hearing, however, I said nothing – after all, it hadn't benefited me the first time.

At this point the judge continued with his thoughts on normal contact, which largely echoed my own proposal of weekends and an annual holiday as fair, before asking me about our son's behaviour.

"Sir," I replied, "Although I profess no expertise in child psychology other than that of being a father and previously raising a daughter, I believe our son is showing the classic symptoms of divided loyalties and a degree of alienation."

I had expected the judge to react to the mention of alienation, but instead he shocked me by declaring that if my son were alienated I would not be able to see him. He said in a condescending voice: "You see, the court has to put the child first and if it is ruled too distressing for your son to see you, you will not see him, do you understand?"

"Yes sir, I understand," I replied, still reeling from the judge's explanation that the emotional abuse of our son could assist Jane's wishes of him not seeing me. I had, a few days prior to this hearing, read about parental alienation in a twelve-page report entitled *A Guide to the Parental Alienation Syndrome*, by Stan Hayward, FNF (Families Need Fathers). This report made me aware of the loophole and the mockery of the law it really is. I had been prepared for Jane's solicitor to stoop low enough to mention it to her, but I regarded it as reckless for the judge to say it under the circumstances.

The judge then turned to acknowledge the CAFCASS officer, a slightly built, twenty-something woman who had been silent throughout the proceedings. "I advise a CAFCASS report for both Jane and Thomas to attend," he said, then gave a suggested schedule of events to have mediation in progress and the CAFCASS report ready for September 7, just under three months from the hearing, and another hearing for September 27 to "move things forward". I knew it would take time and the judge did look at me to ask for my understanding. I acknowledged that I accepted the agenda but questioned what the rules would be for contact in the meantime. The judge looked thoughtful for a moment and proposed an interim hearing for August 9 to "assess progress". I feared my point had been missed, and asked, "But what about contact meantime, sir?"

The judge responded that I "have a court order already in place", which confirmed to me that he had not read my application to the court at all. Somehow, I remained silent, either through shock or fear of contempt. Looking back, all I needed have done is adopt an inquisitive tone and say, "But sir, the current order is not being upheld", but the words eluded me and I kept my mouth firmly shut. With fake smiles and equally false pleasantries, we all drifted out of the room.

As I got back to the waiting room, the twenty-something CAFCASS officer introduced herself as Amy and directed me to an adjoining conference room. I informed her that five years earlier I had gone through an extensive CAFCASS report and that officer seemed to have the full measure of Jane. Unfortunately though, she had since resigned due to depression and CAFCASS does not keep records for that length of time, and so I was back to square one.

Amy questioned me on my concerns about my son's behaviour and I informed her of a number of incidents and situations, such as my son eating with his fingers despite being almost six years old, and that I was unable to influence his table manners with a few hours of random contact. It was also difficult because I did not want to spend most of my time with him continually correcting him, and when I did insist on him using cutlery he looked sternly at me and said, "My mummy says it's okay."

Amy pondered for a while and suggested I take him to somewhere like McDonald's, "where eating with fingers is perfectly acceptable."

I responded with the question, "So you are advising me to accept my son's behaviour and to give his mother the ammunition to accuse me of feeding him junk food?" She looked thoughtful once more and I think she was genuinely trying to find a compromise, but I felt the need to explain that I was not being obstructive, rather I was illustrating the opposing stance Jane would automatically adopt to prolong the charade of keeping me from my son. A silence followed, and I shared a different scenario: "So my son and I had a great day together," I said, explaining how we had gone to the beach and the fun fair before meeting a friend of mine, another Sunday Dad and his two sons. We all had terrific fun until it was time to go home, when my son started saying, "I've not had fun today. I've not enjoyed myself." "If that is not a child with a problem then what is it?" I asked of Amy, and continued: "When we arrived at

Jane's house my son turns to me and says, 'You don't give my mummy any money and you should be giving me money each week,' finishing with, 'Have you got enough money for me to go to Disneyland?' When he was in sight of Jane he turned and hit me, looking at Jane with a broad grin on his face looking for approval. Do you need a degree to see what is happening here?"

Amy had no further comments, so I left the court to walk home in disbelief of the judge, the system, and the appointed CAFCASS officer. I was bitterly disappointed and reminded myself on the entire journey home that much of my disappointment was with myself, because I believe we are all responsible for our own actions and so I am responsible for letting Jane into my life.

When I returned home that afternoon I phoned the mediation services and attended an initial interview, naïvely hoping, once again, that the process may progress as quickly as possible.

CHAPTER 3

After the hearing, contact continued to be defied despite the court order and the judge's statements. When I tried to talk to Jane I would receive a text message stating, "Our son says he does not wish to see you while the legal proceedings are on-going." No six-year-old would say such a thing, and it was an indication that Jane was either lying or burdening our son with every detail of the court cases. Either scenario amounted to emotional abuse, so I wrote to the court:

Dear Sir or Madam,

I regret to inform the court that despite appearing before [the] District Judge on 21 June 2005, contact with my son continues to be frustrated and he has failed to attend any contact sessions as agreed within my court order.

I would therefore be grateful if the review date, currently set for August 9 2005, could be brought forward.

I received a reply just a few days later, which informed me the date had been brought forward to July 21. No more than three hours later a text message arrived from

Jane, in which she asked me to reconfirm my travel dates because her and David would be away as of July 20. I sensed that this was another delaying tactic and so checked the school calendar, which confirmed lessons did not cease until July 22. I then decided to write to the school to enquire if any formal request had been made by Jane for our son to be excused from school on the last two days of term; a reply stated that no request had been made. Nonetheless, I later received another letter from the courts advising that the July 21 hearing had been cancelled and it had reverted to its original date of August 9. Jane had lied yet again and managed to prolong the agony further, but, despite the evidence, no one was even slightly interested.

In the three-month period of June to August between the court hearings I did not see my son at all. Any attempt I made was met with the same response: "He says he does not want to see you until this legal process is over." When August rolled around there had still been no word from CAFCASS and when I called the mediation service to enquire what was happening I was informed that Jane had arranged her first visit with them to take place a few days before the court hearing, which meant yet further delays. So much for me thinking things could progress at any speed.

On August 9 I dutifully returned to court, and a different judge was presiding. Amy was not there; in her place was a tall, slim, middle-aged bespectacled man waiting for arrest by the fashion police in his aging off-the-peg dark grey/blue suit.

The hearing began in much the same fashion as it did before, with Jane insisting visitations had not occurred because our son had stated he did not want to see me.

The judge asked for a summary from the CAFCASS officer, who, red faced, stammered an excuse that the report had not begun because they understood mediation was to first be given a chance to work. These words caused me to suppress further outrage as no such statement had been said in the previous hearing and the nervous response of the officer made it obvious that they had messed up.

As though he already knew the reason and perhaps trying to alleviate the pressure from the officer, the judge looked at Jane and asked why our son did not want to see me. He did not allow time for a reply before suggesting that our son do as he is told rather than dictate the situation before turning back to the CAFCASS officer and saying, "Well something is going off here and it's down to you to get to the bottom of it please." For-malities were concluded and we left the courtroom displaying false pleasantries again.

When we returned to the court reception area, the CAFCASS officer directed me into one of the small con-ference rooms, where, without an apology or eye contact, he explained why the report had yet to be started. I dis-missed his story and said I understood he had a heavy workload, but on the hearing of June 21 the judge had said the report was to be ready for September 7, so how could that be completed in time if mediation was to be tried first? I also pointed out that mediation was tried years prior with no success. Wanting to avoid admitting that he had made a mistake, he assured me the report would be ready for September 27. The due date was actually September 7, but out of diplomacy I did not press the issue. We parted company with him assuring me he would arrange for me to see my son "soon" at the CAFCASS offices.

In the middle of August I received a phone call and a letter confirming a time and date for a CAFCASS visit. I attended a meeting the day before I was due to see my son, and we discussed my concerns about divided loyalties and the signs of alienation. I explained that I was apprehensive about the contact if Jane was to be in the vicinity because it would hugely affect his behaviour, and I was informed she would not be present. Five years earlier I had undergone an identical report and Jane annoyed the attending officer by refusing to leave the room. They reached a compromise that she would sit outside the room but that the door would remain open. The impact of this was that as I tried to spend time with my son, Jane's mobile received several calls and conversations were held at such a volume that everyone could hear. This was not mentioned in the report.

It is not intended to be, but the CAFCASS system is a humiliating process, although it does also offer a chance to spend time with the children. Essentially what happens is that parent and child are in the meeting room, which has some basic toys available. While interacting, the meeting is overseen by a liberal, condescending sort who, according to the government, is suitably qualified to decide on the fate of the parent, child and their relationship. The inevitable humiliation and embarrassment that occurs during the report must be endured and suppressed so the child cannot misinterpret those emotions towards the system as being feelings towards the child itself. The most ironic – or hurtful – aspect was the fact that by the time this report occurred, my son had been on numerous holidays with more than one of his mother's boyfriends, and none of them had to undergo a report or otherwise prove themselves capable of looking after a young child. Yet I, the natural father, was having my background scrutinised in fine detail and despite having nothing to give cause for concern I was still unable to see my own son. Unwittingly, the CAFCASS system is a weapon that can be wielded and is open to abuse by any vindictive parent who has custody of the child.

For this particular report, the CAFCASS officer and I agreed a time the following day for supervised contact with my son at the CAFCASS offices. I arrived on time and was thrilled to see him already playing – it had been arranged for him to arrive early, and Jane was nowhere to be seen.

Having spent no time with him for three months and also being aware that he had likely been told what was happening and how to behave, I was expecting a frosty start to the meeting. In anticipation, I had borrowed two computer games and, laptop in hand, walked over to him. "Hello, son," I said with a big smile, and was delighted when he smiled back at me, albeit silently. In an attempt to avoid any awkwardness, I immediately showed him the games and offered him the choice of which to play. Typically, I am not the biggest advocate of computer games. I believe today's generation can be simply summed up with, "Kids don't climb trees anymore." Nonetheless, he chose his game and he easily outsmarted and outmanoeuvred me, which was ironically exactly what would have happened were we climbing a tree. Laptops take time to start and games take time to load, and those were precious minutes that were passing. I seized the opportunity to have some father-son small talk; after so many weeks without his company, it was a very special moment for me.

We were both squeezed onto a chair and I cannot recall any time when I was so content to continually lose a game. With only an hour of each other's company arranged, I had been concerned about how to end the game and have some less distracted time with my son, but as luck would have it, forty minutes of Spiderman hammered the laptop's battery and we could not play it further. What wasn't so lucky was my son leaving the chair we had shared, walking to another and immediately informing me that he hated me. What struck me the most were not the words, but the calm and matter-of-fact tone in which they were delivered. It did not sound as though he meant what he said, and I do not believe he had any concept of what it meant to hate; I thought he had been prompted to deliver that line.

I decided to ignore the unpleasant remark and continued to unwind the computer cable. In a tone that made it sound like a challenge for him, I asked him to locate a plug socket. He instantly searched the room, hunting one down before declaring with a big smile and that air of a small boy pleased with himself for impressing his dad, "Here's one!" His mind had already forgotten his previous words and his glee with successfully performing my task indicated that it had been a baseless comment.

I plugged the mains cable into the computer and went through the start-up again. My son asked me if we could play Spiderman for a little longer, and accepted it with no fuss when I told him that we didn't have the time. On the computer desktop was a small photograph of my father. I clicked on it to open it and asked, "Who's that?"

"Paul."

"Yes, Granddad Paul," I said.

"No, Paul," he insisted.

I was not surprised at this; although I had not drawn it to anyone's attention, I had noticed that about a year earlier David had decided to stop calling my father his granddad, instead just calling him by his first name.

Our time had come to an end, and I offered a high five. He declined. We both said goodbye and I added that I loved him very much.

With the meeting over, the next hour was earmarked to discuss the contact. The CAFCASS officer was upbeat.

"It upsets me very much hearing that," I said, deliberately avoiding what upset me and expecting his reply.

"No father wants to hear a son say they hate him," he said.

That wasn't what had upset me. "Any child might say that. But only a child that is being influenced against his father stops calling his grandparent Granddad."

This particular officer had been in court with me when I had told the judge my concerns about alienation between my son and I. Jane had told the court she wanted contact to occur and that it was our son who was refusing them, and the judge had responded that a child of that age do as he is told and instructed CAFCASS to get to the root of the problem. I felt that the small incident about the photograph illustrated what was going on. With some further discussion, the CAFCASS officer assured me that, despite his holiday plans, the report would be ready in time for the hearing on September 27, so I returned home. The short time I had spent with my son had reaffirmed both my fears and hopes; he was being heavily influenced against both myself and my family, but he also knew who we were and we had shared some precious and spontaneous moments of laughter. Most importantly, he was, and we were, okay.

A mediation appointment took place in late August. Aside from the one-hour supervised contact, it was several weeks since I had last seen my son and I was in a very cynical frame of mind. Being in the same room as Jane was torturous for me, and when she started speaking every word out of her mouth was either a lie or distortion of the truth. When I asked her why my mother had died without being allowed to see her grandson the glare in her eyes matched the madness of her words: "Because that was what you wanted." Foolishly, I lost my composure. Once again I had been led to slaughter and still had not learnt my lesson. My anger reached a point that the mediator ended the meeting. I left the building ashamed of my failings; I was a fool for letting Jane into my life.

In early September I wondered when the report would be ready. Each morning I would eagerly check the post, but it was always absent. I had made no secret of the fact that I was going to be out of the country for two weeks in the middle of the month, and when my departure came and the CAFCASS report still eluded my letterbox, I reassured myself that it would be waiting for me when I got back.

The holiday itself was a welcome distraction and relief from the ensuing drama at home. It was a cruise around the major Mediterranean cities with the best of friends. A couple of years earlier, Annie, a lifelong friend separated from her husband. In a twist of fate we became more than friends and on the cruise ship we were an item, we embarked on a romance fit for a film script.

When I returned home the CAFCASS report was not amongst my mail, but there was a letter from the courts explaining the September 27 hearing had been pushed back to October 18 "to give CAFCASS time to finalise their report." So much for the officer's reassurances that it would be completed in time but, disappointing as it was, I was currently immune to excess heartache thanks to falling in love with my best friend. I could wait a few more weeks.

Quite what I expected from the CAFCASS report I'm not sure, but I hoped it would confirm that there was no reason for me to not see my son. When it did arrive, I was disappointed; it was entirely on the fence and did not lay blame in any direction or propose any means of moving forward. Jane and I were both criticised mildly and there was emphasis on the need for us to communicate. It smacked of being cautious to not ruffle feathers in case Jane and myself suddenly came to our senses; the only positive thing from the report was that it did not suggest the court cease the contacts, although with the sole exception of the one hour in August there had been none for six months.

When October 18 rolled around and we went to court, the CAFCASS officer and Jane's solicitor shuffled between conference rooms to broker an agreement that was regarded by everyone besides me as a "progression of contact". During the hearing, the judge sanctioned reintroducing time with my son, just a couple of hours a week at first, building up to the original seven hours each Sunday that had been ruled six years prior. I bit my lip as the judge praised us for making such a compromise – he ignored the fact that I had filed the court papers after three years of supposed seven hours a week with my son, during which time contact had been frustrated and stagnant. The purpose of my filing the papers was to enforce the existing ruling on contact and to extend it to weekends and a holiday, so it was difficult not to laugh at his suggestion that this was a compromise. Rather, it was exactly the same condition that had already been ruled and was being broken. The judge then requested that we all shake hands and plan to start anew.

Essentially I was being asked to display my personal wish of putting everything behind us and starting from scratch, and while that's exactly what I wanted to do, I knew it was not something that would be forthcoming from Jane or her family. I did, however, take some joy in the principle of leaving the court and openly shaking hands with both her and her father; when we entered the reception area I walked over to Jane's father. His face showed alarm, clearly he didn't know what my intentions were, but I quickly extended my arm to offer a handshake and said, "We have agreed a future for David, so let's all do our best to make it happen eh?"

"I should bloody well think so," he replied in a not-so-soft tone.

I declined to respond to his comment and instead shook the hands of Jane and her solicitor. With my display of willingness completed, I left the room feeling nauseous. I was well aware that a thousand handshakes would not make peace between us. As an ex-RAF officer and civil servant now in his eighties, Jane's father saw me as the bounder who got his daughter knocked up and wasn't willing to do the decent thing. In a bygone era his point of view would have been justifiable, ironically the same era during which a father had a say in his child's life, but times change and my interpretation of a bounder is someone who emotionally abuses his grandson and denies him the love of his entire family. The love that every child deserves.

Chapter 4

The first contact as ordered by the latest court hearing on October 18 was a two-hour meeting scheduled for the last Wednesday of October 2005. I had learnt from past experience not to attempt contact with David at either Jane's house or her parents', so instead I arranged to collect him from the CAFCASS offices with the officer overseeing.

I arrived on time and entered the very same room I had been in during the last visitation in August. Like last time, David was already there, but he was not happy. The CAFCASS officer, David and I sat for a few minutes to discuss where we wanted to go to tea and what we should do in the two hours we had, and it was explained to David that I would take him back to his mummy's house afterwards. I stood up to leave with David and he burst into tears, defiantly saying he did not want to go anywhere with me. I sat down again and his tears subsided, followed by an emotional weep and the explanation that I had hurt him in the past so he did not want to be with me anymore. Calmly, I asked when I had hurt him, and between sobs he said that I had once hurt his arm when I had held it. I still cannot recall such an incident, but it was instantly obvious that things were going nowhere and I could tell that he had been cruelly manipulated to such a degree that I would never be able to get past his barrier in the short space of time the court had ruled. I gave him a hug, which was not reciprocated, and told him that I loved him very much and would always be there for him. The officer and myself did not need words in that moment, we simply nodded at each other and I left the room.

I believe that the sight of a child suffering such wicked influence would break the heart of any responsible person, but when it is your own child, its mother the influencer, and you are powerless to do anything, the emotion is extreme. Two years prior I had been there when my mother had died; I held her hand as she took her final breaths. I had been powerless then too but there was nothing anyone could do other than give the best palliative care. I was now bordering on the same intense emotion, the difference was that it was possible to identify and treat the problem, but who would or could?

I had by this point been told repeatedly to give up the legal process and walk away. The advice was often from good friends who had the best of intent, but now, so far on and with my son so used and hurt, I could see there was no hope. When I did have contact I had let the frustrations go in the hope that Jane would mellow over time. Perhaps my friends were right, if I walked away then she would not be able to hurt me anymore. Maybe she would even change once her father died. Certainly, stopping the legal proceedings would take David out of the firing line, and it had never been my intention for him to be hurt in any way, but that was what was happening. That evening I decided I had to stop; there were other options, but each of them except one was illegal, and that was the only one I was prepared to pursue.

The following day I went to see my father and informed him of my decision to stop the legal proceedings. He looked relieved and offered his support and understanding, and added, "Your mother would have agreed too." It wasn't until the day of my mother's diagnosis that I had realised how emotional my father was. It had always been taken for granted that they loved each other, but it had never registered with me just how much. He was amazingly caring and attentive during her final few months, and when he was out of the room on one occasion Mum said to me, "Your father has been a wonderful husband; I could not have had a better man." In a family of gentle sarcasm and ribbing humour, these were moving words. I had questioned my father's ways, as any son has, but I had always respected him. He had worked hard for many charities and was a governor of the local school for children with special needs for nearly two decades. And here he was, sat in the chair my mother had traditionally commandeered, a novel from the library laying face down on the table as we drank tea and I received his blessing to give up the legal fight to see his biological grandson.

Just minutes after I left my father's house I received a call from the CAFCASS officer, who wanted to discuss the previous day's attempted contact. My emotions overtook me; I had been able to deal with the frustrations as they occurred over the months, but now they had mounted and overwhelmed me. Parked a hundred yards from my dad's house with my phone pressed to my ear, I wept. The officer understood and I told him I wanted to stop proceedings. He stopped me mid-sentence and told me what had occurred after I left his office the day before. Jane had been in a room downstairs and when the officer returned David to her she said, "I thought you were going with Daddy?" The officer told her I had left the building, David smiled at her and she said sarcastically, "Oh dear."

"Judge Jones should be presiding on Tuesday," the officer told me on the phone. He was the judge who had sanctioned the current contact order. "If you hand deliver a letter of explanation to the courts today I am sure it will be in time to get her back to court for then."

Obligingly, I composed myself and drove home to write the letter, which resulted in a summons to appear in court the following Tuesday. That weekend I wrote in my journal:

After many restless days and nights spent worrying, I have concluded the best course of action is to withdraw my application of the court. It is an agonising decision but the only one I see that will halt the abuse on David. Following Wednesday's contact I cannot permit the emotional beating David is going through to continue. I do not feel it is my doing; I am not the one who is telling him everything and poisoning him, but my actions only serve to fuel the abuse. The court process has done nothing to help, contrarily it has actually made things much worse, and I have no alternative. There may be a wise king sitting in judgement but I hold no breath in hope.

When Tuesday rolled around I arrived early and sat patiently. Jane was there already with her father, and when her brief arrived they disappeared into a consulting room. The CAFCASS officer arrived after me, which was a relief to me because I had worried he would not be present. I had met him the day before to discuss my concerns, and I felt there were two options: the judge must either separate David from Jane, or do nothing and let me disappear from his life. I could see no other alternative.

The CAFCASS officer took me into a conference room and started to talk about the attempted contact where I had left. He said Jane did not agree with the forced approach to seeing David and that it should occur spontaneously. I had heard it all before, but I did not want to argue in defence so I raised an eyebrow and reminded the officer that I had tried this countless times before. Exhausted, I asked how it was possible for anyone not to see what was happening right before them. In the past six months the court order had been denied countless times and I had text Jane every week to ask to see my son, so spontaneity had been flatly rejected. The officer looked at the floor in silence, which reconfirmed my decision to stop the legal battle. The silence dragged on and I had concerns that the officer might think I saw this failure to see my son as a failure on his part. While I was disappointed with his performance concerning the delay in completing the report, I did not hold him responsible for Jane's actions; I looked him in the eyes and with a calm tone said he was a good person and I recognised that within the parameters of his job he had done the best he could for David. I reminded him that I had never been a sycophant to him and assured him I was not doing that now either. I apologised for the times I had snapped but asked for credit that I had called it as I saw it.

When we left the room shortly afterwards Jane's brief approached me. "Can I have a word?" he asked.

"What's the point?" I replied.

"I have some suggestions from Jane," he said and led me to a corner of the room. "Jane has proposed a number of contact sessions where she will be present and supervise the contact."

"Have you not worked out what all this is about yet?" I asked. It was plainly clear to me: the issue was about control. Like her father, Jane must have control at any cost, and by proposing this she could honestly say that she had offered me contact with my son but that I had refused. I was concerned about that briefly, but mentally exhausted and beyond caring what she would say; I knew that no matter what I did she would always insist I was wrong. What was comforting was knowing that everyone around me understood the situation, and a close friend of mine, and a father himself, had told me that I had pursued this far longer than he would have. My own father had pleaded with me to give up because he could see the emotional toll it was taking. My partner Annie had given me her unconditional love and support. I had the backing of all my friends and family, which Jane could never change, so I felt stopping proceedings was the only thing to do for the sake of both David and myself.

The usher called us through to the hearing room and, although still steadfast about withdrawing my application, I was heartened to see that the CAFCASS officer was right and Judge Jones was indeed presiding. Jane's brief once again railroaded the introduction and I sat in silence as the situation seemed to be discussed from every angle bar mine, the biological father's. Judge Jones requested the CAFCASS report and the officer read aloud from his file while the judge took notes.

Finally I was given my say. Distraught, I stood and, deciding talking man to man was required, said quietly, "I applied to this court in May of this year for help and in doing so have actually made things worse. The application was to request the then existing order should be respected and adhered to with the appeal that progression to a weekend and holiday might be possible. At the time I advised the court David was being manipulated and abused. Since then matters have gone from sad to tragic; the court has therefore proved itself inept. I have seen yet more emotional bruises appear on my son and the sight of him last Wednesday at the CAFCASS offices would have broken anyone's heart. The emotional crap is being kicked out of our son and regardless of who is guilty of doing this to him, it is in his best interest that I stop these proceedings. Sir, I withdraw my application to see my son."

A long silence followed. Jane's brief looked amazed. Judge Jones eventually broke the silence and in an emotional voice asked, "This must be a very difficult decision for you to make?"

That was an understatement. "The shittiest decision I have ever had to make in my life sir, but I have no choice."

There was another long silence.

Judge Jones changed his position from leaning across the bench with his hands clenched to sitting back in his chair with a raised posture. "You may have started these proceedings, but you are not at liberty to end them. That right is now in the hands of the court and I am not willing to let you give up on your son."

I was incensed. Fully aware of the risk of being held in contempt of court but too angry to stop myself, I slammed both of my hands down on the desk and in a raised voice declared, "I sir am not giving up on my son, I am giving up on this inept process."

I was expecting a reprimand for my outburst, but rather Judge Jones simply raised his hand to silence me and, to my utter amazement, he apologised and expressed understanding with my frustration with the system and said he understood I was not giving up on my son.

I clarified to the court that I saw my relationship with David as going "on hold" until he decided to seek answers in the future.

Judge Jones then spoke again, "I am putting you under a court order, ordering you to see your son, do you understand?"

Looking back with hindsight I can see his intent, but at the time it just seemed so ironic. I should have kept my mouth shut, but instead I raised my arms in a gesture of exasperation and said, "That's great sir, now please make it happen."

The judge was now clearly annoyed, and the court-room atmosphere had changed. He turned to Jane and derided her by saying she was not fit to be a parent. His body language, manner and tone left no doubt that he was extremely annoyed, and I started to wonder if something drastic may occur from this hearing after all. He continued: "I don't know if it would be best that I take your son away from you."

Jane's heart clearly sank and she broke into tears. My heart also sank, because I knew that if he was genuinely considering such a thing he would not threaten it first, he would just do it. "Perhaps I should order your son be given to his father?" he continued.

Another option to erase, I thought, and continued to cross them off in my mind as the judge presented various forms of punishment that were nothing more than veiled threats.

The judge said that our case was one of the worst he had ever encountered. He spoke of a few stories he had of other proceedings, repeating a few more times that a change of residency may be a good consideration, but each time he quickly moved onto the next subject and it was obvious Jane had now caught up with my realisation that he was not serious in taking such an action after all. He asked the CAFCASS officer for his opinion on the matter, but he did not mention that I had told him my home and lifestyle were suitable for me to look after David, that I would encourage and ensure he had a proper relationship with his entire family, and that by staying where he was I could not see the emotional abuse ending. Rather, it was more akin to a casual conversation until the judge ran through more options, which included psychiatric reports and even David his own legal representation. He made out like he plucked his final order from the sky and, after explaining his reasoning, said that David, Jane and myself should meet in town outside of a shop and I would buy all of us lunch. We had to make it fun for David.

I questioned this decision, relaying the fact that I had concerns about meeting anywhere without an independent supervisor because Jane had falsely accused me of assaulting her on multiple occasions. The judge accused me of being obstructive and informed me I had to comply with the order. I was taken aback at this, because my past experiences were seemingly irrelevant, and all the court orders Jane had defied went unmentioned. Judge Jones had given Jane exactly what she wanted; she had supervised control, and I was under a court order to endure it.

The next morning, after yet another restless night, I found a forum for fathers. It gave me the ability to vent my thoughts and ask for advice, and quicker than I could imagine I realised that I was not alone. There were many others out there in the same situation, and many had stopped long before I had even entertained the idea of doing so.

I spent most of that day trying to find the positives in the ruling from the day before. I pondered over what the judge's motive in his thinking may have been. He came across as someone who genuinely cared and he could see what was going on, and so I thought he must have spotted something that I was currently blind to. The good news did eventually come through to me though: I was not the bad guy anymore. Jane could no longer say I was fighting her through the legal system, because I had tried to back out and the judge had forced the legal system onto us both. He had made it clear to Jane that if she did not stop her emotional abuse of our son and end the deadlock we were in then there would be much worse to come, but the question was whether or not he meant it. Sadly, even if she believed he did mean it, she would easily bypass Judge Jones. After all, she had previously lied about her schedule to delay a court hearing, and there was no reason why she couldn't do the same again and get in front of a different judge the next time.

I was not confident that things would change.

CHAPTER 5

I believed that Jane had always wanted to have control over me, and David was the only means available for her to have it. I was frustrated with the fact that the court order forcing me to attend contact had given her what she wanted, which was to control the relationship I had with my son. As difficult as it was going to be, I had no choice but to do my best. Besides, if this attempt failed then it could make things worse for her, and David would surely suffer no further abuse in the meantime, at least no worse than he had already experienced. I had long maintained that if Jane was given enough rope she would hang herself, and maybe that was what the judge was trying to do.

The contact was to begin the following Saturday and we all attended the first two, after which another hearing was scheduled. We met in town and with it being winter we were governed by the weather on where we could go. I would buy a comic book for David and I to read about the superheroes and complete the quizzes, and we all went to either Pizza Hut or a nearby café. We would visit a local arcade with tenpin bowling and various interactive games. David and I discovered the shuttle board, and it thrilled me to see him having fun within a few moments of playing. What was particularly notice-able was that when he was relaxed he shed all of his self-conscious behaviour around me, which proved that if he was occupied and out of sight of Jane he could be himself without worrying that his every move was being scrutinised for approval.

As already mentioned, another directions hearing took place after two contact sessions, in front of Judge Jones again. I was unsurprised that, after doing exactly what was requested of me, Jane made no offer of increasing contact between my son and myself. I suggested an increase to the judge, but this was not acted upon. I also requested David get his own representation, but that was also declined. It seemed nothing I said in court was ever agreed to. Instead the judge decided to continue the two-hour supervised contact sessions each weekend until Christmas and another hearing on January 10. Judge Jones mentioned that we may want to speak to the York Centre for Separated Families; it was a mere suggestion and there was no mandate to attend, but I took the number. Jane informed the judge that she did not want the contact details because she was already attending a course on assisting children with behavioural problems.

The following day I called the York Centre for Separated Families and spoke extensively on the phone to a woman called Diane. I also travelled to York for an hour and a half meeting with Diane, during which time she made sense of David's behaviour throughout our on-going contact sessions. It was extremely comforting and reassuring to hear her confirm what I had always held true. Her thoughts on his behaviour lifted my spirits and self-esteem a little. She also proposed that I make up a schedule of intended contact leading up to me having him overnight and for an annual holiday. She felt certain that progress could be made and the judge would go along with me.

The contact sessions continued until December 24, as per the order. Christmas contact with David had never happened without an incident and I was expecting more of the same this year. The first Christmas after Jane had left me, my family and I were allowed one hour of contact with David under the supervision of Jane's parents. That contact was to take place the Saturday before Christmas and my parents and daughter had all accompanied me to Jane's house. She watched our every move, and if she left the room for even a moment her father would replace her. When we left the house my mother stated that Jane and her parents were all "off their rockers"; that statement was validated most strongly when we were later accused of hurting David's head and finger and "giving him impetigo", all apparently within the space of one hour and while under extremely strict supervision.

The following Christmas's contact was decided after a lengthy court battle and was to be Boxing Day from ten o'clock in the morning to five o'clock in the evening. We all knew that this would be my mother's last Christmas, as she had received her diagnosis of being terminally ill in September. Nonetheless, moments before midnight on Christmas day Jane phoned me, sounding drunk, and told me that contact would now be from midday to four o'clock, because David was ill and she didn't want him out in the night air. She did not acknowledge my assertion that ten o'clock in the morning was not night air, so I asked what illness he had contracted that would reduce his contact by three hours. This received a response that it was my fault because I had taken him to an indoor swimming pool in October. Ridiculous as it was, I dutifully obliged and turned up to collect him at midday on Boxing Day. He seemed to be in perfect health, and Jane and I had a heated telephone conversation to negotiate him staying a further thirty minutes with me.

So past experience had taught me not to get too excited for Christmas contact with David, and I was vindicated once again in 2005 when we were due to have the next two hour contact. Just before we were due to meet I received a frantic phone call from Jane, and the following is the account of events that I later provided to the court.

At 11.49am I was walking to meet Jane and David at midday at the agreed place. Jane phoned me to say she would be delayed because David had been sick, and I agreed to wait. About ten minutes later Jane called again, demanding to know my location. I informed her that I was in a shop adjacent to where we had agreed to meet, choosing a comic book for David. In a reprimanding tone, Jane told me she was parked nearby and needed help "urgently". She was panicking and blamed the stress of David having to meet me that day as the reason why he had vomited. I walked to her car and saw David in the front passenger seat, and Jane was standing beside it. I opened the driver door and spoke to David, who silently stared at his mother rather than respond to me. He was pale but seemed fine otherwise and there was no sign of vomit on him or within the car. Nonetheless, Jane was adamant that she needed help, so I closed the door and walked around the front of the car. The outside of the front passenger door had a streak of what looked like pale vomit and Jane was trying to clean the panel with some baby wipes. I couldn't see the need for panic or to clean the outside of the car; I asked if David was in a mess and Jane replied that he wasn't. I then suggested we take him for a walk in the fresh air, but I was reprimanded once again. I waited quietly at the front of the car for Jane to finish but she yelled again that she needed help, each time getting louder and attracting the attention of other people. I again suggested taking David out of the car to get some fresh air, and Jane screamed at me: "David is ill for God's sake!" It was clear that nothing I could say or do would help, so I advised we wait until the following day, Christmas Day, for the contact. Jane then advised I ask David if he wanted to see his daddy on Boxing Day. His eyes never left Jane's as he replied that he didn't. Out of eye- and earshot of David I told Jane that she was being obstructive, and she again shouted: "He is ill for God's sake, I need help here!" This time, though, an old male friend of Jane's appeared, and she asked him to explain to me that David was ill. I put my hand on her elbow in a show of support and she screamed, "Take your hands off me!" I asked her to tell her friend that David had vomited because of the pressure of meeting me, but she refused. It was at this point I questioned the coincidence of Jane's friend happening to be there, and I decided to leave. The time by then was approximately 12.15pm.

At 10.17 the following morning I sent Jane a text message, and in the absence of a reply by 11.20am I called her mobile, her landline and her parents' landline, all of which went ignored. At 11.32am I called Jane's parents' home again and this time her father answered. I enquired as to whether Jane and David were there and he replied that he did not know. I sensed an obstructive tone, which wasn't abated by the following comment: "You have a damned cheek wanting to see your son after the performance yesterday." Knowing that if either Jane or David was in hospital or otherwise seriously ill he would know of it, I wished him a happy Christmas and politely ended the conversation. Once again the festive period had resulted in a frustrating lack of contact, but this time Jane had managed to have the short period of time in the car park overseen.

That incident was the start of things to come again, as the sessions scheduled to occur over New Year did not happen. In the middle of the month, when it seemed contact was going to take place again, I arrived a quarter of an hour early to see if I could find anyone who may be there to spy on us this time. Within moments I had spotted another male friend of hers, close enough to be visible but far enough to not be too conspicuous. Having time to kill before Jane and David were due to arrive, I walked into a shopping centre and noticed the same man from outside standing behind a kiosk talking on his mobile. Resisting temptation to go and stand behind him to hear what he had to say, I instead tried to call Jane. Her phone was engaged. I waited for her friend outside to finish his conversation and then called her again. This time, the call connected. I ended the call before she answered. Maybe it was a coincidence. It is a small town and no doubt she received plenty of calls. Then again, the idea of it being a coincidence was slightly discredited when on the exact moment our scheduled meeting was to start the man moved to a position closer to ours and stayed there for several minutes until the three of us went into a café, at which point I lost sight of him.

On January 10 I turned fifty-one and, if memory serves, it was my nineteenth appearance in court regarding contact with my biological son. I had obliged the wishes of Jane and the orders of Judge Jones in appearing to each of the two-hour contact sessions, so I felt I had appeased everyone concerned. I had followed the advice of Diane from the York Centre for Separated Families and created a proposal of scheduled contact between David and myself. It was a simple proposal of a couple of hours per week, gradually increasing to a few more hours a week and in a few months incorporating one overnight visit a week, which was mainly similar to what I had been requesting for years, and I knew that if Jane gave proper encouragement then David would be fine with it. I was under no illusion that Jane would volunteer such an offer, but I did hope that if the judge ordered it to happen that she would comply. I was quietly optimistic that Judge Jones was aware of the reality of the situation. I knew he was in touch with the Centre for Separated Families for one thing, and he had been the person to suggest we attend the group, which I had done and Jane had not. I was also attending a two-hour evening class each week to help separated partners and their children on such issues as understanding and handling the divided loyalties children often have in post-separation situations.

Nonetheless, the reason I was quietly optimistic and not just optimistic is because Judge Jones was one person, not the entire system. I knew that Jane could try to delay proceedings again to face another judge and we would be back to square one. As we entered the hearing room, all my hope dissipated as I saw that Judge Jones was not there; instead, we were before a face entirely new to us both, Judge Renhold. The CAFCASS officer who had witnessed first-hand her behaviour at the attempted collection of David in November and who had been on the case for six months was present in the courtroom, but I knew that it would make no difference. Without Judge Jones, this hearing would be more of the same.

Jane's brief started the process once again. Memory fails me for his exact words, all I recall was that he was attired in the same suit he had worn each time I had seen him. His closing words are the only ones that have remained in my mind: "My client does not see that any increase in contact can be foreseen in the near future." An increase had not been "foreseen in the near future" at any point in the past five years, which I hoped would raise a warning flag for the courts to see that something was amiss.

Before my invitation to speak was offered, the judge asked Jane why contact could not move forward. Evidently the question caught her off guard because she replied with an unrehearsed, ineloquent response that I was verbally abusive to David, and I called him names, and, and, and . . .

Judge Renhold turned to me for a response to the allegations. I denied them, and suggested asking the CAFCASS officer what he knew of our case and how I was with my son.

"The CAFCASS officer has not been present at these past contacts, so what can he report?"

I wanted to say, "Ask him anyway" but I knew I could say nothing that would have any credence, despite the fact I had done nothing wrong. At an earlier hearing the previous November I had said to Judge Jones, "I just do not know what I have done wrong here. Tell me and I will correct it."

His reply was both reassuring and frustrating: "You have done nothing wrong Mr Moore. It is how the system is."

"I am bewildered by this process," I had said further.

"Believe me Mr Moore, if I was in your position I would be equally bewildered."

There was no doubt that Jones was the man for the job. He knew what was going on, but he was not in front of us today. The judge of this day asked me if I had anything further to say, and I put forward the proposed schedule of increased contact as Diane had suggested. It was dismissed immediately, and we left the court with the same two hours a week contact supervised by Jane.

CHAPTER 6

One of the attending fathers at the Centre for Separated Families had advised me that David's school would have its own Social Services worker. It was a concern of mine that David had missed about a third of his schooling from the previous year and had so far been absent for approximately twenty per cent of his current term. What was most worrying was that of everyone I had discussed this with no one seemed remotely interested. I had informed the CAFCASS officer that David was being taken out of school for holidays under the pretence of illness, to such a degree that notes on his school report had read: "Let us hope David will not be so unfortunate as to be so ill next year." I had contacted the school and their social worker got in touch with me; during the conversation it was acknowledged that David had indeed missed a considerable amount of school and it had not gone unnoticed.

We arranged to meet in town a few days later, and in that meeting I discussed my concerns that there appeared a pattern: David seemed to suffer from an illness at similar times to our scheduled contact. The social worker told me that since our conversation on the phone she had spoken to Jane, who argued that it was the stress of seeing me that made our son ill. I shared some of my experiences and asked how the pressure of a court case to establish contact could affect a six-year-old boy unless the pressure was being purposefully applied. I also predicted his next illness: "I guarantee he will be ill immediately preceding either his or my travel plans. He will be too ill to see me before I leave or if he is due to travel he will make a miraculous last-minute recovery." I don't claim to be psychic, but it wasn't a difficult prediction to make given that it had happened five or six times already.

What I was most concerned about was that if I was able to predict his illnesses, and if there were real symptoms that could be diagnosed by a doctor, then there was a chance he was being abused physically. I therefore needed David's doctor to be aware of the pattern of illness, but I knew a doctor would not listen to me in the same way a social worker would.

A few days later, February 21, we were back in court. I was disappointed again because Judge Jones was not presiding, but it was the same judge from the first bout of this round of legal proceedings. He was the same judge who had essentially told Jane how to affect David by telling me that "if your son has been alienated, you will not be getting to see him", but perhaps he would now see the distance I had come and move things forward.

Wearing the same suit and tie, Jane's brief again started proceedings. Once more he asserted no wish to increase contact. When it was my turn to speak, I asked for contact to be moved forward and if that was not possible then the court should recognise the need for David to have his own legal representation. Not a single word was uttered in referral to increasing contact, and in the true spirit of a man destined to continually put his foot in his mouth the judge said, "This court must put the best interests of the child foremost and I am reluctant to order his own legal representation, not least of all because it will cost a considerable amount of money." I recall him stating it could cost "at least five thousand pounds." I saw red at his contradiction particularly so as I had about three weeks earlier paid my income tax, which was more than the figure he had mentioned. Nevertheless, I had learned from past appearances to keep my mouth shut in court and so that is what I did, and we left the room still continuing two-hour supervised contact sessions. I was dejected, to say the least. The same outcome would have been reached if I had stayed at home that day.

My ever-growing contempt for the Family Court Legal System was compounded further and now included the blinkered judge that had presided over that hearing.

As David received no substantive encouragement from Jane the contact was extremely difficult. There was an occasional weak "Come along David, Daddy is here to see you for a little time", completely void of any sincerity and was clearly uttered for my benefit rather than David's, but in saying it Jane could always later say that she had tried to encourage David. Diane and the rest of the staff at the Centre for Separated Families remained a source of inspiration and great help, and I had come to understand fully why David was so shy and permanently seeking approval and support from his mother. As a result of my understanding I had also acquired knowledge: I knew, for instance, to say nothing when he ate scrambled egg in public with his fingers; after all, what chance was there of me influencing his behaviour in a two-hour contact session, especially considering his mother was right there watching us? I had also learnt that if I did try to say something or encourage correction of his table manners, it could be used against me in court that I was "bullying" or "forever getting at him" as Jane was wont to accuse me of.

David would sometimes want to go online to play games on the BBC CBeebies website. He had previously done just that at my home where I had a broadband connection and he could have played all day if he had so desired, but with the supervised contact we had to go to the town library. Each computer there had a notice: "Only two people at a time to each computer please". Coffee was served at the entrance to the building, and so it would have been a perfect opportunity for Jane to retreat for a short while and show that she was promoting contact occurring between father and son. Instead of doing such a thing, she would make a beeline for a computer and sit beside David, forcing me to stand beside them, acting as the third wheel while suffering the glares of the librarian.

Contact was not being promoted in any meaningful way besides turning up. There were moments, however, of genuine father and son time. It was never much – brief eye contact with a smile or a shuffle as he sat beside me, with no prompting, to explain a super hero's special powers from that weekend's comic.

I had learned to accept his behaviour. None of this was his fault, and it was not my place to try to change anything; it would only be used against me in court. So I relished those fleeting moments, the golden minutes that rose from an otherwise frustrating two hours. I was comfortable knowing that he knew who his father was, and Jane could not change that. He knew I wanted to see him. All Jane could do was influence what David thought of me, and I knew that at some point in time that would eventually slap her in the face.

Chapter 7

On April 4 2006 we were in court once more, and facing another new judge. Jane was still refusing to budge on allowing further contact, but it was finally conceded that David should be appointed his own legal guardian and legal representation. It was a relief for me to hear the judge pass the order, but I was floored when he looked confused as to how to go about it, and began to leaf through a very thick fine-print book, which from my angle appeared in the region of ten times bigger than *War and Peace*. As I looked to the CAFCASS officer, my honest recollection of the moment is that the judge then asked, "How exactly do we go about this?" That shock was nothing compared to Jane's brief then having to explain the process to both the judge and the CAFCASS officer.

We all exchanged our travel schedules for the upcoming months and left the hearing room with false pleasantries again. The CAFCASS officer directed me to a conference room.

"Would you have any objection to me being David's legal guardian?" he asked when we were seated.

I did not reply immediately; I had no knowledge of the procedure and had reservations about his abilities since I had known him. I felt as though he had not kept to his promises regarding the original report, and he did not have an assertive manner, something I felt essential when dealing with Jane and her father. I shared this information with him but concluded that he knew the case very well; my reservations were largely removed with the thought of explaining the situation to yet another new face who had no clue of what we had been through. At this time I believed the officer was competent and he was by no means a bad person, he just wasn't as strong-minded as I would have liked. He thanked me then stood up and left the room, explaining that he would be back in a few minutes.

After a quarter of an hour I needed to visit the men's room. On my way down the corridor I passed the usher's desk, and enquired where the officer was.

"Oh, he's left the building now."

Did I just make another decision I'd live to regret?

I received a phone call from the school social worker two days later, which was Thursday 6. It was the first time I had heard from her since our meeting back in February. She told me that since our talk and her subsequent chat with Jane, David's attendance had been perfect – he hadn't missed a single day. Then, in a guarded tone and a noticeable hesitation, she said: "Until today that is. It would seem David is absent from school today because he is ill."

I made no secret of the fact I had long been cynical when I heard David was ill, because the information came too regularly with no substance. "Surprise, surprise," I replied, and suggested she check his travel schedule. She said that she was never given a travel schedule. "I have one, and I'm quite sure he has something booked for Sunday. I will give you a call later when I have checked at home."

The list confirmed my suspicions: David and Jane were due to be away. I called the social worker back to explain the coincidence. "A shilling says he's too ill to make any contact on Saturday 8 or any time this weekend, and another shilling says he will make a miraculous recovery to meet their travel plans."

Right on cue, I received a phone call the following evening, Friday, from Jane to say David was ill and would not be making contact the next day. "The doctor is concerned David is dehydrated."

"Can I see him at any other time then?" I asked.

"We are going away and may have to cancel our travel plans for Sunday."

The next day, Saturday 8, was the scheduled day for our contact. I called Jane in the morning to ask how David was, but there was no reply. I heard nothing all day until 10.30pm, when she called me to say he was "a little better." I asked her to let me know if there was any chance I could see him before he left, but there was no reply.

I called her mobile at lunchtime on Sunday. It clicked through to a continental ringtone, so she was evidently out of the country and must have left not long after she had phoned me the night before. As I had predicted, it was another miraculous recovery from David at the eleventh hour. That evening I sat down and wrote a letter and copied it to David's legal guardian, Social Services, the headmaster of David's school, the CSF and the County Court. The letter explained:

Dear Sir or Madam,

I would be grateful if you could register my concern for my son and note on his records an apparent routine/pattern to his health that fits around our schedule of contact.

Discounting the possibility that information I am being given by his mother may not be correct, and without malice, I am deeply concerned that should his symptoms on these occasions be genuine, there is a possibility he may be being subjected to some form of physical abuse.

What I wanted was someone, anyone, to acknowledge that my ability to predict David's illness and recovery meant that there had to be a reason. Given that I am not psychic, the reason must have either been that Jane was being deliberately obstructive and lying about his illness, or that David was being made to be ill through physical abuse. One could argue that it could have been a coincidence. I would accept that if it had occurred just once or twice, but six times in two years suggested to me that it could not be coincidental.

I hand delivered the letter to David's doctor on the morning of April 10 2006. To this day I have yet to receive a response. I also hand delivered my letter to the CAFCASS offices the same day, and it was marked "For the attention of David's Legal Guardian". I followed that one up with a phone call to the office on my return home, to be informed that the officer in question was on holiday and the only other person that could assist me was in the main office some forty miles away. Coincidentally, though, the woman I spoke to on the phone worked for the Child Contact Centre, which happened to operate from the same building. We had met previously and she was aware of our case, so I informed her what was written in the letter and asked that she do whatever she was able to do to help. She said she would fax it directly to the main office and have someone from there contact me later that same day. As with the doctor, I have yet to hear anything back.

I wrote another letter to CAFCASS and again followed it up with a phone call, except this time I rang the main office. I was passed through several people before finally being told that the person I needed to talk to was on the phone, but that she would call me back immediately after ending her call. Luckily I wasn't waiting by the phone for it to ring, else I would still be there today.

Not all of my letters were ignored. The one I sent to the school social worker received a reply just two days later, wherein I was informed that they were not concerned, although I was told "people are taking notice." That was nice to know, but it would have been even nicer had they made themselves known. The net result from my letters was that after one month I had received only one reply, from the social worker, and she was doing nothing that extended beyond courtesy.

What was particularly frustrating was that everyone around me knew exactly was happening – a mother being obstructive. The entire history of our case proved that to be the most likely, nay, only, explanation possible. I did not need vindication of this, I merely wanted someone in authority to acknowledge the same thing I and everyone else could see. After all, if they can't see what's right in front of them then why should they have such prestigious roles in society? Yet they never did acknowledge it. The closest was Judge Jones, but his seeming understanding of what was happening did not change the situation for either David or me. I was infuriated that there was such indifference from all I had written to, especially as each was a person who should have cared about the welfare of a child.

I had a mild yet nagging concern that maybe David was genuinely ill when Jane said he was, and that this was the result of physical abuse but in such a manner that a doctor would merely brush it aside as a stomach bug. I had to explore this possibility and did a search online for how to induce vomiting. Innumerable links to websites on anorexia appeared, many of which explained how to do that exact thing. While I will skip the detail here, it is incredibly easy to do so, with simple contents from any kitchen. For a child in particular, it would be as simple as someone they trust presenting them with "something that is good for you".

While it was true to say that there was no love lost between Jane and I, I didn't want to think of her as someone who would abuse her own child. Nor did I want to think of David, my own son, as being a victim of abuse, at the hands of his mother no less, yet it seemed possible. It was my understanding that the school social worker represented Social Services, and could advise them of the situation. However, she told me this was not entirely true, so I went to the local Children's Social Care Offices and explained the situation to them. They instructed me to write a letter with dates, instances and other relevant information. I followed instruction; I had dates and instances, and while I lacked actual proof my hope was that alarm bells would ring once reading a list of concurrent coincidences. I received a prompt reply but it was of total indifference. The professional advice was to contact the CAFCASS officer who was assigned to the case – who happened to be the same officer who had ignored my two letters and telephone calls.

I wrote to Diane from the Centre for Separated Families in York to ask her advice on the current situation. I relayed the events of the contact that had occurred and how Jane had blocked it prior to her holiday. Diane agreed that Jane was being obstructive in every means she could. She went on to tell me that Jane had been unwilling to visit Diane's office, even though I had offered to pay for the fuel for the journey, and that during lengthy conversations on the phone Jane had denied David had any divided loyalties between his parents. I suggested that this was a major issue confirming Jane needed help, with which Diane concurred. She carried on by saying that Jane had also told her that it was the stress of both the legal process and having to see me that was making David ill, which was a confession that she was putting her child through her problems. However, Diane also expressed concern that I could be setting myself up to be branded a troublemaker if I continued writing letters that pressed people for answers, although I felt I had already been condemned as such anyway. I felt that the case was beyond hope. While it was reassuring that Diane had accurate observations, she had no legal power and was as powerless to resolve the situation as I was.

Annie and I had a holiday booked for two weeks on May 7, and I had come to terms with letting David go, despite the possibility of the courts ruling to the contrary. I knew that regardless of what the order was, his mother would torment David.

During one of my first evening classes with the Centre for Separated Families in January, Diane had handed out multiple informational fact sheets, one of which was "Bill of Rights for Children Whose Parents are Separated". This sheet contained twelve suggestions from two Family Court judges with years of experience. The suggestions were:

1. The right not to be asked to choose sides between their parents
2. The right not to be told the details of bitter or nasty legal proceedings between their parents
3. The right not to be told negative things about the other parent's personality
4. The right to privacy when talking to either parent on the telephone
5. The right not to be cross examined by one parent after spending time with the other parent
6. The right not to be asked to be a messenger from one parent to another
7. The right not to be asked by one parent to tell the other untruths
8. The right not to be used as a confidant regarding the legal proceedings between parents
9. The right to express feelings, whatever those feelings may be
10. The right to choose not to express certain feelings
11. The right to be protected from parental warfare
12. The right not to be made to feel guilty for loving both parents

When I was handed the paper I had considered David was receiving no such rights. However, the heading atop the sheet read: "These are not actual legal rights". As

I see it, the law's stance is to hide behind the pretext of "To always put the best interest of the child first", yet it accounts for none of the twelve points. I once again saw the hypocrisy we were all embroiled in, the futility of the legal process and the indifference of the people who had a duty of care to the children. I could see no other alternative than to stop David's torment by stopping the legal process and trying to regain my contact to him. With the heart-breaking decision made, I decided to try not to dwell on it and so attempted to overlook the mess of the previous weeks and look forward to the upcoming holiday.

Days before we were scheduled to leave for the holiday I received a court summons to cover the issue of failed contact before Jane's own travel in early April. Both Jane and I were instructed to appear in court, but she was further instructed to provide decisive evidence to support her reasoning in not making that contact. The order was dated April 11, which would have been the day after the courts received my letter, and Judge Jones had signed it but according to the postmark it had taken a full three weeks for the court to process it. I visited the courthouse to enquire if all was correct, as it would mean cancelling my holiday. The courthouse confirmed it, and when I questioned the timing to process the clerk appeared to be unsurprised with the delay: "It's the start of holiday season; we're busy and understaffed."

I toyed with the idea of writing to inform the court that I would be away but, going against my friends' advice and with Annie's full support, I cancelled our flights. My gut feeling was that somewhere, someone had taken note as the school social worker said they would. My cynicism went into temporary remission and to avoid Jane using my holiday as a delaying tactic I sent her a text message to let her know that I had cancelled it.

On the weekend a messenger from Jane's brief's office hand delivered a large brown envelope to my house. It contained a statement to the courts with a letter from David's doctor and a list of patient history, as well as a receipt for medical expenses from a doctor in Portugal. The extensive statement confirmed David to be too ill to make contact on Saturday April 8, but Jane thought by two o'clock the following morning he was a little better and a holiday would "do him good". According to the Portuguese medical note, though, her judgement had been wrong.

When the day of the hearing came, I arrived early and expected there to be the usual back and forth with her brief talking to the CAFCASS officer, the officer to me and so on. This was standard procedure for us but had never reached a resolution to us moving forward. The officer entered the waiting room and was acknowledged by the usher before walking over to speak to me, asking how I was.

His question took me aback; I took a deep breath and told him in a calm but firm tone that I was disappointed he lacked the decency to reply to my letters.

His eyes did not meet mine as he nervously remarked he was surprised that no one from his office had contacted me.

This did not appease me, and I recalled his failings from when he had first been allocated David's case, finishing with: "And now you're his legal guardian and you choose not to reply to my letters or telephone calls?"

"I'm not David's guardian," he answered meekly.

I was stunned. It was now nearly five weeks since we had spoken in the conference room and he asked if I would agree to him being David's legal guardian; I had heard nothing from him since and now he was telling me that responsibility had gone to another person.

"We had a meeting a couple of days after the last court hearing on April 4 and Bob Cronin was elected as David's guardian," he informed me.

I was utterly shocked at this and calmly told him that I considered both him and the legal process to be damned incompetent.

We entered the hearing room and I saw yet another judge, this one female. Jane's brief began: "This order of the following application by Mr Moore—"

"This order was requested by the court, sir, not Mr Moore," the judge corrected. At last I had been defended by the system.

Jane's brief continued his speech, giving reasons for failure to make the contact and referring to the letter and medical history from the doctor. When he was finished the judge looked to me and asked for my response.

"Do you think it extreme that David was too ill to see me at any time of day on Saturday but was well enough to travel at two o'clock the following morning?" I asked.

"The doctor's letter confirms that your son had gastroenteritis, are you dissatisfied with the facts?" she responded.

"Yes ma'am, I am dissatisfied. In an earlier conversation with the social worker of my son's school I predicted that he would be ill on that day, and more pertinently I also predicted he would make a speedy recovery in time for their planned holiday. I feel that if

I can accurately guess my son's illness then there is surely reason to be concerned."

"Mr Moore, the court has been presented with confirmation from a medical practitioner that your son was ill, and that should be enough to satisfy all concerned."

"I am not suggesting that the note is fake, but if a doctor is diagnosing an ailment that can be easily induced, ma'am, then I believe there is even more cause for concern," I said.

The judge dismissed my comments but appeared to be sympathetic to my cause.

"I request of you that you make a note, that the pattern of my son's illnesses have appeared six times in the past two years," I stated.

The judge appeared to write something down and the hearing was then brought to a close.

As I left the courtroom Jane's brief approached me and enquired into my travel plans. Jane would relish the fact that I had cancelled them.

"I will be leaving tomorrow to resume my holiday, which means I will be missing the two upcoming contact Saturdays as planned," I explained.

The people in the waiting room, including Jane and her father, overheard this conversation, and Jane said she was not sure of the Saturday I was returning, which happened nearly every time. Another prediction of mine to come true.

"Tell you what," I said, "why don't you call me when you think you are willing to let our son see his father?" and promptly exited the court.

Once outside I called Annie.

"How did it go?" she asked.

"A waste of time. I should have told them I would be away on holiday and delayed it. Give the travel agent a ring and let's get out to the boat straight away."

Within seven hours we were on our way to the airport. The adrenaline coursing through my body made driving through the night an easy enough endeavour, and in the morning we lifted the boat's anchor.

"Time to try and forget," Annie said.

I looked at her and smiled. "I love you very much." As I looked out over the water I added, "And I love the escape this little sailboat gives me."

A couple of days later we dropped anchor in a cove that I had often passed but never ventured into. Annie rowed a line ashore so we could safely moor overnight. As the sun retreated behind the horizon and the moonlight shone down on us, its shape was mirrored in the calm and glass-like sea below, enhancing the tranquil scene that enveloped us. "I could stay here with you forever," I said.

"I could stay with you forever too but we'd need to leave this place at some point if only to restock the tonics."

We looked at each other and smiled. She was the woman I had known for many years as a best friend, but I knew in my heart she was the woman I wanted to spend my life with. She thought so too, and we returned to England engaged.

When I opened my front door on returning there was a letter from CAFCASS sitting amongst the rest of the post. The postmark was two days after the last court hearing, when I had reprimanded the officer. I opened it and found inside a letter from Bob Cronin officially introducing himself as David's legal guardian. Within the letter he requested that I call him on his mobile phone directly, the number of which he had included. I did so the next morning only to be told the number was wrong. I called CAFCASS to explain the mistake and asked for the correct number, and was informed that they couldn't give me his direct number. After toing and froing about how I could contact him, I suggested that I read out the number he had provided me and the person on the other end of the phone tell me what was wrong with it. They agreed.

"One digit too many," they said.

"Thank you. Which one is it please?"

Reluctantly, they told me which one to delete. I tried to call it again and while it was indeed a real number, the phone was turned off.

"I hope this isn't a measure of things to come," I said to myself.

CHAPTER 8

There was an occasion, when David was only a couple of years old and I was in the early stages of trying to get access, when I was listening to the radio on a long road trip. The big story in the news was the development of a contraceptive pill for men, and presenters from seemingly each station were getting much mileage from it. Many news reports were ending with the story and the almost universal approach was that of amusement, which I found bewildering. From what I could hear, no one was reporting on the major issues in the development and marketing of this pill, not least the possibility that it may increase the practice of unprotected sex and the damage this would have on the many years of educating people about sexually transmitted diseases. I also recognised an advantage to the male pill that had not been mentioned, namely, that my situation would have been avoided had it been me on the pill rather than Jane. I knew I was not the only man to have fallen foul of a woman who lied to her partner about taking the pill in order to become pregnant.

Then the phone-in began.

I had been driving all day and while I, too, saw the amusement at the presenters' suggestions that men can't remember things at the best of times, let alone taking a pill every day, my annoyance had been building at the lack of serious reporting happening on the issue. When I was an hour from home a late night national station got onto the topic, and the presenter gave the number for the public to call in with their thoughts. I dialled the number and to my amazement I was connected.

"Hello caller, you're through to the live show, what's your name?"

The question caught me off guard. I knew exactly what it was I wanted to say regarding the topic, but I now had similar feelings to when I would suffer intense nervousness when I had to speak publicly in front of large audiences. On the spot, I replied and gave my real name like an idiot, not knowing how much detail might be divulged. Before I had time to find my composure the second question was fired.

"Where are you from?"

Once again I gave the actual town in which I lived. It is a small town and there was no one there who shared my name, so the consequences could have been quite serious.

"So what are your thoughts on a male contraceptive pill?"

My immediate response was far more lucid than my last two: "Beyond the dangers of increased potential for unprotected sex, I consider that a male contraceptive pill will offer the single most effective contribution to safeguarding a man's integrity since the invention of the glass bottomed tankard."

"What are you on about?" the presenter asked, in a tone that implied I may not be entirely sane.

"The glass bottomed tankard?"

"Yes," came the reply in the same tone.

It then dawned on me that his voice was that of a man half my age, and the chances were that the majority of listeners would be younger than him. I needed to explain what I meant. "In the old days, if you drank from a tankard that had a coin thrown into it you were immediately press ganged into the navy. So someone came up with a glass bottomed tankard, which enabled the drinker to see through and check there was no coin in there before drinking from it."

"Yes, and so?" the presenter was still using the tone that implied I was slightly crazy.

"So a male pill will give a man the wherewithal to ensure he can't be shanghaied." I realised he probably wouldn't know what that meant, so before he could recommend I see a psychiatrist I explained what 'shanghaied' meant: "Entrapped, snared, tricked into parenthood by a woman with a hormonal body clock ticking like a time bomb and a schedule she is determined to stick to."

I was finally making sense to him. His attitude and voice changed, and he spoke to me in a more respectable tone. We talked further as he clawed back esteem from the listeners by sharing my concerns about the continued need for condoms, not solely relying on a contraceptive that will not prevent sexually transmitted diseases.

The downside was that I had identified both my name and my personal issues to a large audience, but nothing untoward occurred as a result. There was another radio broadcast a while later that inspired me to write to my local MP:

Dear Sir,
Driving home at the end of a long day I was listening to the radio. A social worker was speaking of a heroin addict who had beaten up his

pregnant girlfriend and the success in convincing the girl to press charges against him. A conviction with a prison sentence for a violent drug abuser and the father of the unborn child. Had the story ended there I may have continued to nod my head in approval, but the story concluded with a new-born child and the state ensuring that the father have contact.

I was raised with traditional values. My mother taught me to work hard, save, contribute to society and try never to burden the state. This I have done, I have assets and pay taxes. I get no help in trying to see my son and my mother died without being granted one minute with her grandson in her own right as a grandmother.

I was not holding my breath for a reply but one did actually arrive a few days later, on paper headed with House of Commons. It looked very official and very impressive, with a dark green font and a small portcullis. My MP's response was to thank me for writing to him and to inform me that he had written to the appropriate government department on my behalf. A month later I received a copy of a response from the Department for Education and Skills, Rt Hon Margaret Hodge MBE MP Minister for Children, Young People and Families. The letter was longer than the number of words in the department it came from, but it still said little. It simply referred to a Green Paper that the British Government had recently published, and said that the consultation process was open should I wish to contribute by writing to an enclosed address, as well as a website where I could contribute my concerns.

Instances such as these made it increasingly difficult not to become the cynical old man I used to consider my father to be. There was a quote that I would once have rolled my eyes at: When the job is not up to much, give it a long name. That fact, coupled with the on-going quest for political correctness, was a recipe for many to lose all hope. I wrote my letter and I left my comments on the website. Nothing happened as a result. Whether I have learnt my lesson to stop trying on such matters I do not yet know, but I no longer call into live radio broadcasts.

CHAPTER 9

When I finally did get through to Bob Cronin we made arrangements for him to visit me at home. He was a cordial, articulate and well-dressed man who could easily be mistaken for a salesman if not for his penchant for wearing sandals with no socks.

We discussed the situation for about an hour, which was frustrating because by this time I had lost count of how many different people I had relayed the story to. The problem this posed for me was that as time went by I tried to find a quicker way of getting as much information across as I could, which meant employing the use of metaphors and on this occasion I cut straight to it: "It's like this Bob, Jane is going to pee all over you and you will end up apologising to her for not having an umbrella."

A half-smile emerged on his face and he changed tactic. "I understand you have a photo of Jane's father hiding behind a tree opposite your home. May I see it?"

The photo was amongst the large pile of paperwork I had filed from the case. I found it and handed it to him. He made no comment on it, and instead told me Jane was furious that I had built a garage at my home. She would have known this because construction was still in progress and anyone could see it easily if they passed the house. Nonetheless, my response was probably not the best delivery, but I was annoyed that this was the topic of conversation.

"What the hell has me having a garage got to do with seeing my son?" I produced another file from the stack, which was a letter Jane sent shortly after she left me. In it, she gave me three options regarding money, none of which mentioned any contact with David except the last one, which stated that if I paid the minimum amount I would see him "if and when he chooses to see you later in his life."

Bob then brought up the accusation against me that I was violent.

"I have no record of being violent at all, nor have I ever been accused of such, which Jane could verify. If I was a violent man, I would have been more likely to punch her father for spying on me instead of taking a photograph," I rebutted. Bob did not respond verbally or through body language, so I continued. "Half an hour before scheduled contact Jane called me to say David had slept in, so would I mind picking him up from her parents' house fifteen minutes after the time that was agreed in the court order. I agreed, albeit reluctantly. When I arrived at the house, her father answered the door and with a face like thunder accused me of being late. I told him that I had agreed the delay at Jane's wish because David had slept in. He moved his face to within inches of mine and called me a liar. If I were a violent man do you not think I would have hit him right there?" Bob still did not respond. "When Jane appeared at the door with David she did not confirm my story, rather she looked on with relish that there was conflict between myself and her father. I still didn't hit anyone."

Bob changed tactic again. It seemed that no matter what the accusation was against me, everyone thought I was guilty.

"What about when I returned from a business trip to South Africa, when David was about two years old?" I began. "I bought him a beautiful jacket with the big five animals, cut out of matching fabric and sewed in random places. When I returned David to Jane's parents' home, I put the jacket on him. The next time I had access to him I was given the jacket in a bag with the explanation that David didn't like it. I later tried to put the jacket on him and he screamed; he was very distressed. What had gone off there?" I asked Bob. There was no response. "You know what she's going to do?" I asked rhetorically. "Years from now, when David asks her why she would not allow me to see him, she will heap the blame onto him, saying, 'But David, I was only doing what you wanted sweetheart.' What kind of damage will that cause to him?"

Cronin again remained quiet. He had appointed a solicitor to David: a woman from a law firm forty miles away, who sent me five letters in this period. These letters were an introduction, a letter advising me she was changing firms but would still be handling David's case, and information that she was advising me of legal aid she was claiming for representing my son. She made just one trip to court and as far as I am aware she offered no suggestions to move things forward. I was appalled at how our tax money was changing hands faster than water down a drain with minimal effort and no results. All I could see from this solicitor was complacency and her having a firm grip on the gravy train.

I questioned Bob about David's schedule of illness and asked for a justifiable explanation.

After speaking in detail with the school and Jane, Bob came back to me with his opinion: "It is a combination of David's genetic nervous disposition coupled with that of his mother's." I took that to mean that Jane was making him ill, but Bob wouldn't say anything further on the matter. He then dismissed any further argument by saying: "If you look at the clouds you can see patterns!"

Sometime later the report compiled by Bob arrived in the post. It acknowledged that no matter what I did, Jane would not be happy. It also said that I had agreed to any further work with psychologists or anyone else who could help, but Jane had repeatedly refused to engage in such programmes. However, it had no suggestions on how to move forward aside from recommending I write to David, which they called 'indirect contact'. It also contained no consideration for David's health issues that were continually increasing and were being levied by Jane as a result of the court action. While I had not expected to emerge as the shining star and her as the wicked witch, I had hoped that someone would take lead, as in the true measure of what one would imagine a legal guardian should be. Both the report and Bob Cronin's role confirmed him to be, in my mind, nothing more than a legal observer.

I realised once more that the only protection I could give David from this insanity was to request withdrawing my application for contact. No one was interested in his regular illnesses, there were no suggestions of moving forward, and so I felt there was no other choice.

We appeared in court again in November 2006, and Judge Jones was presiding. David's solicitor kept quiet. Bob Cronin arrived in a suit, tie and barefoot in sandals, reiterating what was in his report. I do not recall Jane's brief saying anything, but if he had it would not have been a suggestion of moving forward. The atmosphere in the room was one of apathy, and when I was finally asked if I had anything to say I said, "Yes sir, I wish you to grant me the right to end these proceedings as I do not believe I can justify pursuing this to be in the best interest of my son."

There was a brief silence, before Judge Jones broke it by agreeing to my request. "Your action is very brave, and I hope normality reaches events in time," he told me.

I didn't think they ever could or would.

I left the building without saying a word to anyone. I added my name to my mental list of people who had failed David, and as I opened the doors to the sunlight outside I felt the state was my enemy. I was given no say in my son's life but was instructed to pay child support. My son's health was being manipulated and no one was interested. This was a gross injustice in my eyes. As I walked down the road I felt betrayed by the country that I had always believed to be the home of democracy and justice.

CHAPTER 10

It was a year on now, and 2007 had been a strange reprieve. I had come to terms with no longer hoping to see David and while I thought of him on a daily basis I was able to console myself by knowing that he was at least not growing up in a place where poverty and starvation are everyday occurrences. I also felt that I had relieved some of the pressure off him by no longer dragging him through the legal system.

The disappearance of Madeleine McCann from her hotel room in Portugal had been making the news for most of the year, and posters of her face were plastered everywhere. Each time I saw a poster or her story in the news I remembered how fortunate that at least I knew where David was. Nonetheless, Madeleine's case stirred issues with me, because there was a global outpouring of emotion but at the same time hundreds of children are emotionally abused and denied access to their families in this very country, yet they fail to make the news. I could never compare the situation of what I was experiencing to that of Madeleine or her family; regardless of the heartbreak of losing my son I could at least hold onto knowing that he was home and safe, just not with me. Madeleine's story was sheer tragedy, and I continue to hope that she will one day find her family again.

Annie and I had decided to wed on July 7, 2007. Part of this decision was our agreement that 07/07/07 would be an unforgettable date – although this logic was quickly deflated as on our first anniversary we both made separate plans for July 7 in advance and had to suffice with an anniversary lunch. I had sent a wedding invite to David in the hope water would have passed under the bridge, but I did not get a reply. I had made a contingency plan to get him a last-minute outfit if need be, but it was futile.

After the wedding we enjoyed our summer immensely, with sailing and plenty of planning. My father agreed to sell his home to move into the apartment below us; we had purchased and refurbished the apartment in anticipation of him moving in and were offering it as a holiday apartment in the meantime. Dad had always quipped to my brother and I that "If your mother goes first you can be sure there'll be nothing left when I pop off because I'll have blown the bloody lot!" Each time he said it we laughed, but now that situation was reality we reassured him that we both had our own money and he should sell the house to do what he had always asserted.

"I know you two buggers are doing alright!" he said each year since Mum had passed as he booked a cruise around Africa or around the world.

He moved into the apartment in September and announced he had booked another cruise in January 2008, with the justification statement of "This time it goes east to west." Not one of us begrudged him; we knew how much pleasure he derived from the cruises, and he and my mother had been on many during their marriage. We later found his diaries from his time on these voyages, which attested how much he missed her while on them, but we also knew that they brought him closer to the experiences they shared as a couple. They were no doubt bittersweet journeys. After informing us of his latest trip to come, he said, "Well I always said I'd blow the lot if your mum went first and when I get back from this next cruise I'll be skint, so the house has to go." Such delivery was typical for my father; it would have been nice to hear that he was ready to move on and be closer to the remaining family he had, but even though his heart was always in the right place he had to deliver his feelings with a backhander.

Backhanded or not, he did have feelings and he could get emotional. He was a long-standing member of the local Lions and was twice the president of the organisation. One of his duties was to stand outside a local supermarket at Christmas time with a collection bucket to raise money for the less fortunate. The previous Christmas, in 2006, he was doing that and saw David, Jane and her parents enter the doorway by which he was standing. His biological grandson had been ushered to the side so he could not see his grandfather as they entered the shop. Dad told me the story later that day, with the memorable ending about Jane's father: "I'd like to knock that old twat's block off!"

In November 2007 I was discussing the whole issue of not seeing David with my daughter. She loved her little brother, but she showed outward acceptance of the insanity we were going through.

"I feel I did my best," I said, referring to withdrawing the court application the year before.

"But did you?" she asked.

Since dropping the legal action I had posted on a related Internet forum multiple times, warning fathers new to the legal system of what I had been through. Each time I had to go into great detail because most replies were simply, "You should never give up on your children." I would counter by asking what they would do if continuing meant the child would be subjected to physical abuse, and if walking away was the only way to stop that abuse. Most of the members acknowledged the impossible situation I had been in, but others would insist they would continue. At that point I would ask if they were truly putting the child's best interests first or actually their own. A moderator stepped in and told me in a private message that although they agreed with what I had said, "We cannot tell them that at the outset. Let's face it, not many of them will be dealing with the kind of mindset the mother of your son has."

Criticism of my decision was par for the course, but I felt justified because I had gone through the process for so long and seen David get torn up. But my daughter questioning whether it was the right thing or not started me thinking again. After several sleepless nights, I decided that, along with a letter to David every other week, the next one would include a separate letter to Jane asking for permission to see my son.

The letter was just a couple of lines long:

Dear Jane,
It has been a year since we were in court, I would be grateful if I could see David.

The reply was surprisingly quick, but unsurprising in its content:

David does not want to see you.

I contacted the Centre for Separated Families again, and made an appointment for the following week with one of the directors, Karen Woodall. Annie came with me, wanting to show support, saying: "Whatever happens now is an affect on both of our lives." She was, of course, absolutely right

Karen has a wealth of experience and many qualifications in family counselling. Along with her husband she has written multiple books on how children are affected by divorce and how to best protect and parent children through the unavoidable difficulty that divorce creates. When we met, Karen listened to my story and asked pertinent questions about what I had been through. She was yet another new face to me, but there was something different about her; there was understanding radiating from her and I immediately liked her attitude: she did not hold back from telling me if I was on the wrong tack, or if I was looking at things the wrong way. Her tone is one of both confidence and gentle authority – I knew I was in the company of someone I should respect, and so I did; it was what I had been longing for the entire time I had been meeting people supposedly working in the best interest of the child within the legal process.

The meeting lasted for two hours, during which time Karen had questioned me thoroughly and made plenty of notes. She was aware that I had worked with the Centre with Diane, who had now moved to different employment, and that Diane's notes on my case were still on file.

Karen then surprised me by mentioning Parental Alienation Syndrome. This was something I had become aware of years before and had subsequently read about it extensively, but as the courts did not recognise it as a syndrome I had refrained from mentioning it to Karen. Not only that, but she mentioned things I had read about and even expressed concerns over possible abuse, which was a statement I was by no means expecting. She then went on to tell me how David may develop should his environment not change – in other words, if he was not removed from living with an intense and overbearing mother. The term she used was "parental enmeshment", a phrase I had never heard before but would hear a lot more of in the time to follow. Karen then told me that there was a good chance David could become a self-harmer as he got older. This resonated with me and I thought of Jane; she had never cut herself to my knowledge, but I occasionally thought she had a degree of the self-harming mentality because she would often create situations that made her look like the underdog and would accordingly generate attention or sympathy for her.

Karen described to me that children who are abused tend to take two possible courses when they come of age: they will either rebel, turn against the parent(s) and not have anything good to say about them, or they will become enmeshed to the point that the parent(s) is perceived as perfect and nothing can be said to challenge or criticise them.

I was taken aback – Karen had just described the two personalities of Jane and her sister.

"Karen, do you think it would be in my son's best interests for me to return to court? I'm in my fifties now and at a complete loss of what will be best for him."

She was adamant that I return to court to fight for access to David.

During the forty-mile drive home Annie and I discussed nothing other than the meeting and what to do next. We decided that the following day I would call David's school and ask them to monitor him because I was going back to court.

I dialled the number the next morning as planned and was immediately put through to the headmaster. Before I even managed to say hello he was talking: "I was expecting to hear from you Mr Moore. David is at the top of my list for concern."

Needless to say, I had no idea what he was talking about, having kept out of my son's life for a year. My call was just to tell him I was going back to court and I hadn't even filed the application yet.

"David has been missing more school due to poor health. His mother has asked that he only attend in the mornings because his strength is low while he recovers from his latest illness."

I informed the headmaster that I was returning to court and ended the call, silently fuming. Despite all the previous concerns over David's attendance in school and the assurances from the social worker that I would be kept in the loop if anything changed, I heard of it only by calling the school.

Enough was enough. I completed the court forms that night and filed them the following morning.

CHAPTER 11

It took a few weeks to process the court application and a provisional hearing date to be issued. I was expecting Jane to try her old delaying tactics again, but, to my surprise, she didn't.

In the time leading up to the next court appearance I had made contact with someone through the fathers' forum I was a member of. This particular member was a McKenzie Friend, which is someone who is not legally qualified but has experience and is able to accompany a person to a court hearing. After talking on the phone and exchanging numerous emails, I decided that she did not need to accompany me this time. Although I was applying to return to court, I had no hope that my request would be granted; rather, the process was more to keep legal action on-going so I could monitor David's health and attendance in school. The irony of the situation was not lost on me though: that a year prior I had withdrawn from the legal process because of the very reasons of David's health and school attendance. The fact remained however that David was suffering whether I was in court or not, but at least in the future if he ever questioned me I could display the court papers to him to show I had always tried to have access to him.

In court, it was the same female judge who had overseen the hearing when David was too ill to attend contact but had recovered enough to go on holiday later that same day. Jane's brief again got to talk first, and kept his opening statement short: "David does not wish to see his father."

That statement never ceases to infuriate me when no one replies with the obvious response: "And given that he hasn't seen his father for years, why do you suppose that is?" Instead of asking such a question though, the judge retained the same expression, wrote something down, and asked of me: "And what are you wanting, Mr Moore?" To this day I cannot think of a more ridiculous question. I had filed papers requesting to see my son, the opening statement had referred to my son and I seeing each other, and yet the judge still had to ask what I was in court for.

"One hour a month, supervised, ma'am," I stated calmly. The judge raised an eyebrow and wrote more notes. She then looked at Jane and motioned with her hands to ask why this was not possible.

"David will not attend if he does not want to," was the reply.

The judge and Jane's brief spoke for a few moments, and the York contact centre was mentioned, as well as its ability to supervise a one-hour contact "if" David could be persuaded to attend. I wanted to enquire why the contact could not occur at home rather than travelling forty miles, but I knew it was pointless – David was never going to tell Jane he voluntarily wanted to spend time with me. Still, the hearing had a degree of success because it ended with us all agreeing to try supervised contact at the Centre for Separated Families in York if David would go. I knew it wouldn't happen, but two things were gained: firstly, the court had ruled at least somewhat in my favour, and secondly, I had a piece of paper signed by the judge that proved I had tried again to see my son.

In early January 2008 I drove my father the three hundred or more miles to his departure port for his world cruise. Each time he would say to me, "I've had enough of flying son, jetlag and all that confined space on long-haul flights. I want to get on board a ship and take it easy."

My response was the same each time too: "Yes Dad, but I have a six hundred mile round trip!"

The routine for dropping him off was very similar to taking a child to school. He was excited in the car to be going, but when we reached the departure lounge it was considered uncool to be seen with the family saying goodbye. As such, the farewells were kept to a minimum, and on this particular occasion they were very simple indeed: "Right son, you get your head down and have a nap on the way back, you must be knackered." Then he was gone. I always looked over my shoulder to see him as I left, conscious that it may be the last time I ever saw him. After all, three months away from home, out at sea no less, is a long time when you are approaching eighty years of age.

Annie had come along for the drive and was now laughing at the farewell.

"Bloody marvellous," I said. "Yesterday he has lunch in town with my brother and his wife, Dad was in tears as he said goodbye. I drive him over three hundred miles and what do I get? Instructed to take a nap! Not even a token offer of money for fuel!" I joined Annie in laughter at the situation. I couldn't help but feel affection for my father, as inconvenient as the journey was for me. We laughed even harder as we relived the stop at the motorway services on the way to the ship. Dad had given me £2.50 and said, "Here son, I'll buy the coffees, you go and get them." We didn't tell him they would cost that much each, not combined, because we knew doing so would incite a tirade about how when he had a café "tea and coffee were only twenty pence a cup," forgetting how many years ago that was.

I'm sure all families have similar experiences, and they all join together to create fond memories that we look back on to remember the personalities of our closest companions.

After just a few weeks, attempts of a one-hour supervised contact session had failed and we were once again in court before Judge Renhold. I had spoken extensively with Karen in the time between court appearances, and she had praised me for requesting only one hour a month. She also complimented my concern and understanding in David finding it difficult in re-establishing contact with me. While I can't deny I enjoyed having my ego stoked, I had to tell her the truth behind my meagre request of one hour a month: "I knew that no matter what I requested it would be declined, so by asking for the bare minimum I knew I could prove my point."

Karen brushed this off. "Regardless of your motivation, my interpretation will be how the judge also saw it, and probably accounted for her raising an eyebrow to you in court."

I bit my lip and resumed enjoying the misguided compliment.

Jane's brief started proceedings again, and explained in a condescending tone how it was regretful that contact had been unsuccessful. When my turn came, I said in a relaxed voice: "Sir, I am here in contempt and all I expect is the paper with your name on it stating that I had tried to see my son."

The judge was visibly annoyed and gave both Jane and I a talking down, accusing us both of being "the most dreadful parents."

Jane said nothing, while I rose to the counter. "Yes, clearly I am. Can you tell me, sir, what it is I have done wrong, sir?" I was having the desired effect of annoying him further, so continued: "And if you can't, can I please see my son sir? And if I can't see my son I trust you will understand my contempt of this legal process?" and with that I threw my arms up in the air in a gesture of hopelessness he had moments before condemned.

"I will not have a father not seeing his child come into this courtroom and throw his arms up in the air in defiant surrender," he replied.

I couldn't resist. I threw my arms up in defiant surrender again and looked him in the eye. He did not reciprocate the eye contact. He said something about the ridiculousness of everything, which I agreed with, and ordered a further CAFCASS report.

Great, I thought, *back to square one with yet one more new face to the case*. I left the room, but this time I had not only the paper signed by the judge but also the pleasure of telling the court exactly how I felt.

On February 14, 2008, Annie and I were packed and ready to leave early the next morning for Heathrow with my brother and his wife for a two week holiday. I spent the evening making some long-distance phone calls to ensure everything was in place during our absence. As I put the phone down after a call it rang immediately, and my sister-in-law was on the other end. In a frantic voice she told me my father had passed away that day while in Raratonga.

"I'm sorry I had to tell you on the phone. The cruise line has been trying to reach you but your line was engaged, otherwise you would have been the first to know."

Annie, my daughter and I had all spoken to Dad on the ship's phone just two days earlier, he had told us what a great time he was having, and told us individually that he loved us. I cannot express the huge emotions I felt at losing my father. I felt shame that both my parents had now died without being allowed their grandson, and that shame of their heartache being my responsibility will stay with me forever. However, there were ironies to his death that will always bring a smile to my face. He had always said that if Mum died first he would spend all the money, and he made good on that promise – his estate was worth barely more than loose change, but he did have credit on his cruise bar tab. His house was on the market to sell, and shortly after he died the cliff-top a few hundred metres from the house collapsed into the sea. The local paper ran a front-page report with an aerial view of the area and a red arc through the areas deemed to be at risk. The line went straight through his house. Apparently his promise to spend everything also included the house!

It was also ironic that he died where he did, in Raratonga. When we got hold of his diaries later, he had written, while on a previous cruise, "Raratonga – don't reckon much to this place!"

In our hearts, Dad will be forever cruising the world. About a year after his death my cousin was in Cape Town when the cruise ship my father had died on berthed for a couple of days. My cousin stood at the dockside and saluted his uncle as the ship lifted the lines and headed to the horizon.

I began to think of the impending CAFCASS report. I thought it should be a simple matter of meeting a new person, who would have read the files CAFCASS already had. Little did I know the hypocrisy I was about to encounter.

I arrived at the CAFCASS offices slightly early and was shown the waiting area. Within a few minutes a middle-aged man with grey hair greeted me.

"Would you like a cup of tea?" he asked.

I politely declined.

"Have you attended CAFCASS before?" he asked.

His question took me aback because it should have all been on file. It is possible he was trying to rile me though – I had written to CAFCASS in the past to complain about the failings of the previous officer, so perhaps this new one was thinking of payback. As he guided me into the familiar room with a cup of tea in one hand and a pen and paper in the other, I answered his question: "This matter has been on-going for eight years and there have been two previous CAFCASS reports. Have you not read up on this case from your files?"

"Oh no, no, no, no," he replied. "I prefer to start each case afresh."

I refrained from saying what he actually meant was that he just couldn't be bothered to do his research, but it's highly likely my facial expression let him know.

So the meeting was not off to a good start, and it got worse when he asked me if I paid my Child Support Agency (CSA) child support. The question stunned me; I had been told repeatedly that child support payments and contact are separate issues. If he actually was trying to rile me, he was doing a good job.

"What has me paying child support got to do with seeing my son?" I asked. "They are separate issues."

"Ah, yes, legally that may be so," he said patronisingly, "but I use it as a measure as to what kind of a father you are." He continued with the outrageous questions: "Do you get off on anger, Mr Moore?"

I could not believe what I was hearing. "What? This issue has been dragged out for eight years. I have appeared in court twenty-seven times, both of my parents have died without access to their grandson, and now I learn that the officer allocated to the court ordered CAFCASS report is not only arrogant, but entirely ignorant of this case." I stopped, noticing his obvious enjoyment of my reaction.

"I do Yoga," he said, continuing to goad me. "I find if I take a deep breath and count to five, then exhale and count to five, then six, seven, and so on, it calms me down."

I knew that showing any defensive emotion was what he wanted, so I calmed down.

"Why don't you leave?" he asked.

"Will that get me contact with my son?"

He avoided the question and instead began talking about the history of raising my daughter and my relationship with her mother after we had separated. There had never been contact issues with my daughter and we had never been to court to decide access. All parties previously involved had told me this was irrelevant, but he was making notes all the time. "If I was to replay a video of this meeting, it would show you to be a most aggressive and angry individual, Mr Moore," he said, motioning towards a corner of the room to simulate where a camera would be.

"Yes, and if I was to replay a recording of this meeting to your superiors, it would show you to be an arrogant antagonist who despite all the rules pitches child support and contact as a joint issue," I then motioned to my chest to indicate where a microphone may be positioned.

That resonated with him. His face changed considerably at the suggestion that he may be recorded. I had no microphone, of course, but he couldn't be sure of that any more than I could be sure he didn't have a camera recording us.

The meeting was a shambles, but I did take away one piece of advice: if I requested it of the court, I was entitled to a final hearing based on the principle of contact. In other words, I could get a ruling that the court agreed I should have contact with my son, but that, in consideration of the distress it would bring upon him from his mother pressuring him, the court would be unable to order contact. I can't think of a more perfect example to display the insanity of Family Law.

CHAPTER 12

We were back in court with a CAFCASS report that offered no recommendations other than a hearing on the principle of contact. We were before the same judge as last time, Judge Renhold, and as Jane's brief again began his patronising speech in his monotonous tone, the judge cut him short.

"This is downright ridiculous," he chastised. "You should both be ashamed of yourselves. Now get out of my sight and do not return until you can tell me which psychologist you are going to work with. Do I make myself clear?"

We filed out with our tails between our legs. In the waiting area I was approached by Jane's brief and led into a private room.

"Right, we need to arrange a psychologist report," he said as though it had been his idea.

"Great, let's go for it," I readily agreed. "I've been in full agreement of a psychologist getting involved since the last legal guardian's report, but your client refused." The last statement invoked a grimace from his face. I continued "But it isn't so much your client that needs the psychologist is it? Rather, her father might be the one needing help; he's a lot of the problem."

"Who is going to pay for this?" he asked.

"I'll pay for my part of the report, not a problem."

"Well . . ." he stopped again. "Jane's Legal Aid has run out, so she is directly financing the costs now."

I was in disbelief, and more than a little disgusted that the brief continued taking the money knowing her situation. "She's spent up the equity of her home to stop me seeing my son?"

"Yes. And you are right about her father, by the way."

The situation became clear. I could pay for the whole report and the court may choose not to act, or I could pay my share and let Jane's side worry about it. Then again, it was possible the court would order me to pay. I decided to stand my ground: "I am happy to pay for my share, but Jane's financial situation is not my problem."

There was a long silence, but I felt that the brief should be the one to end it.

"Perhaps if we were to work with the Centre for Separated Families," he again adopted the tone that it was his own idea.

Bloody rich, I thought. *How many years have I been working with them? How many times has Jane said she will contact them? I've even offered to pay her expenses to travel to York and work with them and she still refused.* I again saw the need to remain silent on these matters and just nodded my head in agreement, and asked him to expand on what we should tell the judge.

I found out some months later that if the court had ordered Jane she would be obligated to finance the report. Her sleazy brief had been trying to coerce me into paying!

We went back to the courtroom and Jane's brief delivered the decision, as though it was a move of dramatic significance that would make it unnecessary to return to court again. Judge Renhold did not receive the information as enthusiastically as it was delivered, but agreed and made some fine-tuning to the wording for the court order. The agreed schedule was that Jane and I would work with Karen Woodall from the Centre for Separated Families with a target of re-establishing contact by June 1 2008.

As I left the court I phoned Karen with the news. I sensed she wanted to get further into the case, so I told her I would be ready to start whenever she wanted.

Karen's enthusiasm is infectious, but Jane's tactic of agreeing to the minimum she could get away with then repeatedly delaying was predictable now. Predictable, but effective. It was therefore no surprise to learn that two months later Jane had not begun working with Karen.

For my part, I spoke numerous times on the phone with Karen and met her on several occasions to speak about where we were, where things should be going, and we discussed numerous possible scenarios that could unfold. Each time though, the emphasis was on David's best interests. The possibility of him living with Annie and I was covered in detail, from how it would affect our lives to what help we would all need to cope with the transition.

I learned many considerations, one of which being how I would handle the situation if David did live with me. Close friends of mine had often said that Jane was raising him in such a way that he would resent her one day for denying him access to his father. I also thought this likely to happen, though she would insist she was only doing what David wanted. I thought I would have to defend Jane to David with excuses like her being ill. Karen dismissed the idea, and insisted that if David was to come to me about Jane and what he had been through, the last thing I should do is demean his perceptions.

Chapter 13

By March 2009, the Centre for Separated Families had drawn up a schedule of approved work. Jane and I had both agreed to it, and the courts had rubber stamped it. Karen Woodall was appointed as mediator, with the intention of finding common ground between Jane and myself so that we could work out how to progress. However, Jane's old tactics were deployed again: she refused meetings with Karen and would only talk on the phone.

By April, I had completed work with the CSF, which had involved attending meetings and discussing in fine detail different scenarios and what, in each case, would be in David's best interests. The process was essentially counselling on how to handle his behaviour as a result of everything he had been through; he was extremely timid and quiet, and I was not allowed to say anything negative about his mother. Rather, I had to be willing and able to engage two-way conversation about Jane and his maternal family. This was an introduction to potential problems I would face with him as a result of him being so alienated from me and being supplied so much negativity about me. To put it simply, my work with the CSF was about moving things forward and learning how to adequately cope with David's behaviour to re-establish my relationship with him. I knew in my heart David held no true recollections of any harm that had befallen him during his contact with me.

Karen was forced to suspend work with Jane after allegations from her about me. Jane had told Karen that the school was not remotely concerned and that I was fabricating the stories regarding David's illnesses. Karen had no choice but to stop working with Jane until she could establish which of us was telling the truth. This scored more time for Jane and slowed down the process even further.

Nonetheless, it was not going to be too difficult to establish the truth: a phone call to the school and another read through the plethora of letters and documentation I had filed soon exposed Jane's habitual need to say whatever came into her mind to delay or derail progress.

Aside from the fact that I had previously raised a daughter, I had fought back my cynicism to attend the CSF parenting classes and very quickly began to realise how much more there was to learn about children and their development. I had by now completed sixty-six hours of experimental learning with the CSF, which entailed an eighty-mile round trip for classes every Tuesday evening. Exercises included the attending parents being instructed to kneel on the floor, where a simulated argument was conducted over, around, even 'at' us with raised voices and dour tones. It was an illuminating mock-up of a child's perspective being spoken to at that height. This lesson hit me like a brick: on top of their confusions and anxieties, children are further intimidated because of the angle at which they see the world, which can hugely exacerbate their insecurity. Another class included drawing pictures of our children; I was not the only parent to draw a figure Lowrey would have been proud of and I believe everyone drew their child's face with a smile on it. We had to write down everything we could think of that was positive about our child. There were a myriad of exercises, all of which had a central goal of providing us with a broader outlook. I left there with a greater understanding of how my son would perceive things, and how children's natural divided loyalties can be so easily open to abuse by those who love them.

On a further court hearing on June 2, the judge ordered Karen to attend the next hearing on July 7. In preparation of that hearing, Karen compiled a report in which she criticised the previous CAFCASS accounts, compiled by the officer who had informed me he practiced yoga. Karen's report was sixteen pages in length, and very detailed. She explained her involvement with Jane and I; for me, she detailed how I had been involved with CSF since 2004, when I worked with Diane. The report mentioned my six-week course on Children in Focus, which was created to heighten the awareness of children affected by family separation, and how I "participated willingly and fully in each two-hour session." It also noted that in 2005/6 I had six one-hour counselling sessions "designed to enable Mr Moore to reduce stress around the lack of contact with his son", three half-day workshops "on understanding the needs of children affected by family separation" in 2006/7, two half-day workshops on understanding empathic parenting skills in 2007/8, and six half-day workshops "on empathic parenting skills, re-establishing parenting after a break, understanding the reluctant child, reassuring the reluctant child, confident parenting after separation and coping with difficulties in contact" in 2008/9.

Jane's involvement was noted to be less taxing: in 2008 she had three forty-five minute telephone sessions "offered as part of a strategy to support the re-establishment of contact" between David and myself; in 2009, one twenty-five minute counselling session "which was halted due to allegations" made by Jane about me; and in 2009 a twenty-minute telephone conversation "which was halted due to allegations" made by Jane about Karen's professional conduct. All in all, Jane's dealings amassed to three hours of phone calls, two of which were halted early as a result of allegations.

Karen's report also noted how she was supposed to interview David from request of the court, and she wrote to Jane with a number of dates that she was free to meet him. After several attempts to have a conversation with Jane, a date was set for meeting with David on the 25th June 2009. On the day before the meeting, Karen telephoned Jane as arranged and asked her to bring David to the contact centre. Jane said that David would not come to the contact centre and that if Karen would not go to their house, he would not see her. Karen discussed the situation with her external supervisor and decided to go to the family home rather than not see David at all. She confirmed a visit on the 25th June at 4.30pm and asked Jane to be available for a short telephone conversation beforehand. The phone call concluded with Jane making allegations against Karen, thereby sabotaging her meeting with David. Karen's report concluded that: "it seemed to be that there was nothing that Mr Moore can do to change Jane's implacable hostility towards contact." It then said that: "This setting did not seem to me to be conducive to any meeting with David, I asked Jane to consider how she could contribute to a more effective environment for the re-introduction of contact".

Further to this, Karen highlighted her worries:

I have some deep concerns about this case. In particular, the way evidence of frustrated and blocked contact may have been overlooked. Jane continued to the present day to assert that she stopped contact because Mr Moore was "rough with David and bullying, critical and insensitive to his needs" and that David now cites this as his reason for not wanting to see his father. However, despite Mr Moore being interviewed by four different professionals in this case, there continues to be complete lack of evidence to support these claims. In fact, contrary to the idea that Mr Moore is the danger, other professionals involved in the case have pointed to Jane's own relationship with David as being a cause for concern.

Karen also spoke of the opinions of others:

A review of the documentation pertaining to the case shows very clearly that concerns have been raised about the level of emotional enmeshment between mother and son, particularly by the Children's Guardian . . . These concerns have been further echoed by David's headteacher. I consider that these concerns, together with the level of implacable hostility towards contact that has been demonstrated by Jane since the parties separated and by David since September 2005, constitutes evidence for further investigation. Specifically, a psychologist's report is, in my opinion, urgently needed . . . so that the court can further understand the issues at play in this case . . . My most recent conversation with Jane only serves to heighten my feeling that there is an active and long-standing campaign on her part to ensure that Mr Moore does not have any contact with David. Jane's responses to the questions that I asked her cause me concern. Jane spoke of David feeling "really scared and anxious" at the prospect of contact with his father, exact words that have been spoken by David to other professionals. Whilst these may be a true expression of his feeling, words and phrases that are repeated in exactly the same way by parent and child over a period of years, can point to coaching and encouragement from a parent to view the other in a negative light.

At long last, after all the years fighting in court, here was a professional who had worked to understand the case and could see the situation for what it really was – and specifically, understood Jane's psychological profile, predicting Jane's behaviour and able to recognise the hurdles being deliberately erected to prevent me having contact with my son.

Karen's report also included detail of the reports from CAFCASS. The first had mentioned that David and I had enjoyed a relationship in 2000, and stated that "it would be beneficial to David to have extended contact with his father". The officer mentioned there had been "no substantive evidence of Mr Moore's inability to care for David, I have observed a positive bond and believe that this needs to be maintained and encouraged."

Karen further noted that in the time between that report and October 2001, I had appeared in Family Court four times to establish unsupervised contact with my son, which started in October 2001 (I had also attended Magistrates Court three times). However, between that time and May 2005, "at least" thirty-one contact sessions "were cancelled, altered or cut short" by Jane, and in the summer of 2004 alone "all but five contact times were cancelled. At the end of May 2005 Mr Moore returned to the court to ask that the original order be reinforced, at which point Jane stopped contact completely."

The second CAFCASS report, in 2005, "showed that David was now hostile to the re-establishment of contact with his father." The symptoms of parental alienation were also showing quite profusely:

David is reflected in the 2005 report as a chatty child who would tend to look at his mother a lot when speaking. Supervision of the relationship between David and his father describes an incident referred to by [the CAFCASS officer] as "bizarre" in which David, nearing the end of his time with his father, turned to him and said "You know I really do hate you."

Rather than bizarre, if this remark is viewed in the context of possible efforts by Jane to alienate David from Mr Moore, the comment by David is entirely understandable. Children who experience parental alienation must make a psychological transition after contact with a targeted parent in order to ensure that the alienating parent does not reject them. One possibility for this remark is that

David was simply adjusting his behaviour in order
to please his mother who was waiting outside.

What was also interesting was the court had failed to
recognise the situation, despite that report also stating
that: "the parties were recommended to work with the
Centre for Separated Families. Mr Moore took up all
offers of support and completed parenting education
courses and attended counselling. Jane did not see any
reason to do so."

Also given mention in Karen's paper was Bob
Cronin's 2006 report. Cronin had been appointed as
David's guardian, and Karen noticed that his paper
"notes that David now calls his father 'Thomas'". It
should be noted that removal of the family relationship
by encouraging a child to call relatives by their given
names is one of the strategies that alienating parents
can employ to undermine relationships." Cronin's report
was quite detailed, and Karen made reference to how
it stated that: "David is reported to have stated this
his father is 'cruel' and that he feels 'really scared and
anxious' when he is with him. These words are repeated by David in subsequent reports and are the exact
words used by Jane to the current day to justify David's
unwillingness to see his father."

It continued: "It is noticeable that David has few
close friends. I have spoken to his headteacher . . . who
comments that it appears that David is wrapped in
cotton wool by his mother." Cronin was concerned that
David was starting to stand out amongst his peers, and
Karen mentioned that "he is seen for example as the
only boy who is brought to the front gate by his mother
holding his mother's hand." As Cronin recommended a

psychologist's involvement to help make decisions in the matter, Karen mentioned that I was willing to participate in this, but Jane refused.

By the time of the latest CAFCASS report in August 2008, Karen knew that I had

> dedicated a total of sixty-six hours of experiential learning with the Centre for Separated Families in order to effect personal change in his relationship with his son. This constitutes in my mind a considerable demonstration of his willingness to change. Jane had completed just three hours of telephone counselling work in which she acted on two occasions to sabotage the input. This suggests to me that the mindset that has to change in order for this to be resolved is that of Jane.

The sixteen-page report was submitted to court on July 7, and as a result the judge appointed David his own solicitor, Adam Davies from a child solicitors' firm. The court also ordered Social Services to do a Section 37 report, which is when a court considers that a Care Order or Supervision Order would be appropriate, and orders the local authority to conduct an investigation on the child's circumstances and then report them to the court within eight weeks.

During this hearing I had remained silent, and I left with my head racing as it had in June 2005. Karen and I went directly to a private consultation room off from the main court waiting area. As we entered, Karen looked at me and smiled; she knew exactly where I was emotionally – I had endured years of madness, heartache, frustrations, false allegations, perjury against me, the failure of the legal process to listen to me, watching powerlessly as my son was being openly abused, fighting a system that by default treats fathers with absolute disregard.

Karen's report had made waves, but that's because she had put so much effort into it. When Annie and I visited Karen's office, it was like stepping onto a set for Crime Scene Investigation. There were about eight flipcharts placed around the room, each one containing its own information from what I had supplied. Karen had gone through my notes and shown visually the pattern of David's health issues. She made the point that if you looked at just one or two, nothing seemed amiss, but if you looked at it en masse then suddenly the pattern would become apparent and, in Karen's words, "alarm bells would ring". It goes without saying that it was a huge relief for me to have someone, a professional no less, know what I was up against, what David was going through, what Jane was suffering from, and on top of that to put such an extreme amount of time and effort into the report.

After nearly ten years the tide had suddenly turned, and I could not hold back the tears.

CHAPTER 14

Social Services allocated to David a caseworker by the name of Tina, and she had filed the Section 37 report by the last day of August. In compiling the report, Tina had conducted extensive interviews with David, Jane and her family, myself and all the professionals who had been involved in David's life. I was not surprised that there were no concrete statements regarding David's individual health issues over the years, but the extent of observations on his emotional wellbeing was damning. James, the Social Services Family Support Worker, had been assigned to work one-on-one with David and had begun to build a rapport, helped by various summer outdoor activities. He had also visited Annie and I, giving us the opportunity to share information and up-dates on David's progress.

We were back in court in mid September, but the format was different to what I was used to: Social Services now took control. While Jane and her father were in a conference room, the Social Services team asked Jane's brief and I to join them in a separate room for talks. Jane had submitted a statement declaring that she was willing to fully cooperate with Social Services in a programme of work they saw necessary for David; I reminded them of Jane's previous agreement to work with Karen and the deliberate frustrations that were used to derail that process. A manager from Social Services then spoke: "If Jane does not cooperate then she risks David being taken from her care."

I rebuffed the remark, and quoted three judges who on multiple occasions had threatened the very same action with no effect. At that moment, there was a knock on the door and in walked Adam Davies, the solicitor for David appointed by Judge Renhold. He was a well-built man in his fifties and dressed in standard solicitor clothing.

He introduced himself, placed an old-fashioned brown leather briefcase on the floor next to him, and effortlessly took command of the room. "Right, what's going on?" he scanned the faces in the room. His delivery was as though everyone here had failed his client, David. His stature was that of someone who commanded respect, and his self-confidence radiated throughout the room. I liked him immediately. He was the man David needed all along, and I do not think it a coincidence that Judge Renhold had appointed him specifically.

Adam Davies enquired what Social Services wanted to happen. After defining several points, he asked for a chronology and associated documentation going back to the very first court appearances nine years earlier.

There was a ripple of concern amongst the Social Services team. They explained they only had information going back a couple of years. Before Adam could say anything, I interjected: "I have everything here," and raised my rucksack, which was stuffed to bursting. The room went silent. "It's all there. Everything, right back to day one," I said.

Adam looked at the rucksack, then me. He remained silent for a while; words were not needed, his eye contact and face expressed satisfaction that I had done my homework. "I'll need to copy everything," he eventually said.

"Of course," I replied.

The court hearing itself was over quickly. Jane agreed with Social Services to their schedule, so all that remained was for Judge Renhold to agree and stamp the paper.

Following the Section 37 report, Social Services decided to start a Risk Assessment for David, which took place on September 30, 2009. The findings were that the basic care offered to David was good, but he had suffered significant emotional harm as a direct result of Jane's care, and that same care was denying his right to a relationship with his father. It was also stated that there were concerns over David's emotional development, identity, social skills and independence being severely restricted by Jane, which could have permanent effects if not addressed.

The verdict put David at a high-risk level and needed Child Protection Services to get involved. His risk was so high, in fact, that on a 0 to 10 scale, with 10 being "safe enough to close the case" and 0 being "no safety", David was ranked at a 2.

At the start of October 2009 I received a letter from Child Protection Services, informing me of the concerns regarding David's welfare. They wanted Jane and I to attend a meeting on October 14 with an extensive list of professionals, some of whom were already involved in David's life. This meeting was to decide whether David should be put on the Protection Register.

The entire Social Services team was present, fully briefed on the situation and each well aware of what was going on. Nonetheless, we all had to endure the frustrations of pedantic attention to detail – as they later privately explained to me, "if we fail to cross every T and dot every I or make a single mistake, it could derail the legal process".

Interestingly, David's school nurse was present; about a year earlier I had spoken to her on the phone about David's illness. I had told her I was able to predict with worrying accuracy when he would become ill, and challenged her that it could not be coincidence. I had pleaded with her, "Please, prove me wrong". She had no comment at the time, but now she sat in the meeting adamant that David was at risk of harm from Jane.

David's doctor was also there, but was not in agreement. Over the years I had written to him on several occasions and never received a reply, so once I walked into the surgery and booked an appointment with him. In that appointment I explained the schedule of illness David was on, and he dismissed my concerns and showed me the door. He ruled out the concerns of Social Services in their preparation of the Section 37 report. Now, in the meeting with Social Services, as the decision went to a vote, the doctor stood up and walked out of the room, muttering words to the effect that if this constituted abuse then half the children in the country would also be at risk. I reasoned to myself then as I had on leaving his surgery that he was only seeing individual events and not the pattern from the chronology Karen had so painstakingly displayed with her room full of flip charts. His vote was academic; David was placed on the Protection Register.

By November there had been many appointments and interviews with Social Services. Annie and I had met all their requests, cancelling and rescheduling whatever plans we had at the time. Jane, in keeping with tradition, was less compliant. Apparently she had made it difficult for Social Services to work with David, with a list of sudden after school activities he had going on, forcing rescheduling or delaying meetings. Jane and her father had argued repeatedly with Social Services, and they behaved as though the entire situation was just an inconvenience to them.

This wasn't the first time the Social Services team had dealt with this behaviour though, and Tina Carpenter called a meeting with Annie and I. She was courteous, efficient, and explained some of what had been going on with Jane and her father.

"One accusation from Jane," she had said to me, "was that your daughter tried to drown David and you had stood there laughing while she did so. Jane and her father also insist David has full recollection of this incident."

Despite it being a ridiculous accusation, Social Services were duty-bound to investigate everything. In doing so, Tina, her boss and Jane's father had a meeting, in which he told them David was less than a year old at the time of the supposed drowning. Tina and her boss responded with the fact that David would not have such a detailed memory of an incident at that age; David's grandfather vehemently argued that it is possible, and he himself has many memories from when he was under a year old.

"I wish someone would understand what is going on here and actually do something about it. David would not suffer like this if he was removed from Jane," I eventually said, unprepared for the answer.

"It's not a question of *if* we will take David into care, it is a case of *when*," Tina replied.

Annie and I were silenced. Social Services knew precisely what was happening. They were following the correct protocol to ensure the proper outcome was achieved, and were every bit as frustrated with the progress as I was. As we left the building, we both looked at each other and said in unison, "Bloody hell, they are going to do it!"

The past few years had brought many changes to our lives, and there was another big change waiting for us: we had discussed with Karen the effect and options of managing with David in our lives full time. It was now looking more of a reality. All Jane had to do to keep her son living with her was to engage with Social Services, but it looked increasingly unlikely that she would do so.

A major concern for me was that I had not seen my son in almost four years, and not spent serious time with him for five years. My recollections of him were as a five-year-old; he was now ten.

We were back in court on December 4, 2009, but this time we were emboldened by Karen's report, the Section 37, the Risk Assessment from Social Services, David being put on the Child Protection Register, and Adam Davies being fully briefed to fight for my son's corner.

Karen had assisted me in writing a statement to the court, in which I explained that it was now nine years since I started court proceedings to gain contact with David, and that Jane had obstructed it at every opportunity with repeated accusations. "All of these allegations have been disproved and yet I am still unable to have any contact or relationship with David because of the on-going efforts on the part of his mother to alienate him from me," I continued.

I went on to mention that it had now been determined that David was considered to be at risk of harm because of the emotional enmeshment he was suffering, and that, while Social Services understood the seriousness of the situation, considering Jane's false accusations about me over almost a decade, "a quickening of the pace of action is urgently needed."

I ended my statement with the assertions that much evidence had been accrued to show David's surroundings were detrimental to his well being, that he was about to enter his most formative years in which most damage would be inflicted, and finally that he should be removed from his mother and I would work with the Local Authority to give him whatever would be required to meet his needs.

By this point, Social Services had uncovered a considerable amount of additional facts and had instructed a psychologist to work with Jane, David and myself to produce a full report. They had further instructed a full paediatrician's investigation and report on David's health issues from birth, with work to begin early in the New Year.

I had been writing to David every other week since Bob Cronin had been appointed his guardian, although Cronin's position ceased when I withdrew my case in 2006. Finding it difficult to know what to say in a one-way correspondence to an alienated son, I had usually given updates on what the family was up to and wished him well in his schooling and activities. James, the Family Support Worker, had established Jane to have my letters in a cabinet out of reach of David. She had reasoned: "David knows when they arrive and where they are, he only has to ask if he wants to read them". Copies of my eighty-four letters were given to all the parties, and Jane had written derogatory or negative remarks about me on several of them. I was embarrassed to see my private words that I had struggled to write each time now being focused on. I was assured the content of my letters was appropriate and caring, but they were required to illustrate Jane's nature. There were several other damning examples Social Services had of Jane's failings as a parent, all of which were to be passed to the psychologist.

The case had now taken a more positive turn but then I was informed Tina was to take maternity leave in the New Year, and a new caseworker would be appointed. The thought of yet another new face to the process daunted me, because it could mean losing momentum.

CHAPTER 15

In January 2010 I had the first appointment with the psychologist, Andrew Green. His office was a two-hour drive away, and as her daughter lived only a few miles from there, Annie travelled with me so we could go out for dinner that evening. We had anticipated the appointment with the psychologist would last around two hours, but it actually lasted double that. Andrew and I discussed the chronology of events from me first meeting Jane up to the present day. He diligently scribbled notes down, asking questions and sharing observations throughout. In his possession were all the files, notes and letters I had sent to David and professionals over the years. He explained his role, apologising in advance of asking very personal and searching questions, establishing that he was not there to judge or take sides.

We discussed Jane's first statement to the Magistrates Court back in 2000, where she had listed forty-two reasons why I should not see David. I produced my counter statement, which a good friend had assisted me in writing out of concern that I was about to be fried in court. Pedantically we had discussed and explained every absurd accusation but when I had presented it to the solicitor acting for me at the time he dismissed the need to file it to the court. Events proved him to be correct, as I had been awarded contact via the

Magistrates, though Jane had disregarded the order. Now Andrew wanted to address the statement and discuss each allegation. I explained to him that Social Services had been through every detail with me; I quoted Shakespeare: "Me thinks she doth protest too much" and affirmed it as Jane's tactic: "Throw enough shit and some is bound to stick". I expressed my frustration that so many of the professionals had looked en-masse at Jane's statement and her subsequent allegations and failed to see them as showing her to be the root of the problem.

Andrew continued to make notes. "Is it true, as Jane accuses, that you refused to buy safety gates for the stairs when David was a baby?"

"Yes, it is true Andrew." I repeated the accusation emphasising each word, "I refused to buy safety gates", and asked him, "But that is only half of the truth, would you like to hear the whole truth?"

Andrew nodded.

"I bought safety gates for my home, where we were living at the time. I also bought safety gates for Jane's house, which she owned and stayed at with David on occasion. However, I refused to buy a third set of safety gates for Jane's parents' house, given that they could either buy their own or the gates from Jane's house could be taken to their home, David was not going to be in two places at the same time. So I *have* to admit to refusing to buy safety gates." I explained Jane's expertise in half-truths, her devious ability to take a sentence and miss a word so twisting it to justify her need.

"She states you wanted to leave David, three months old at the time, on the boat while you went to a restaurant, is *that* true?" Andrew questioned.

"Yes," I confirmed and produced a photograph of the little sailboat I owned a share of in the Med, moored directly outside a waterfront restaurant with a table less than a metre from the bow. "If we had sat in the cockpit of the boat we'd have been further away from David than we were when sat at the table".

Every ridiculous twisted 'reason' Jane had presented in that statement had a perfectly sane explanation.

"He forced me to go on holiday while six months pregnant."

I explained we'd booked the holiday long before the pregnancy was confirmed and Jane had checked with her doctor prior to going. I produced the holiday photos, Jane looked very happy in all of them, and at no point did she express a wish not to go.

"He made David sleep in a damp bedroom."

Social Services had inspected the room. I produced a photograph of a less-than-two-inch light brown shadow a foot or so from the ceiling in the middle of a chimneybreast. I'd had the chimney capped some years earlier, and the spot had never gone.

"He invested thousands of pounds on the stock market."

I presume in this she was referring to my personal pension plan which my accountant would discuss each year. I questioned Andrew, "What has my PPP got to do with me seeing my son? And if she saw us as a permanent item surely she would've been happy to know I was investing for the future?"

I was not afraid of addressing the entire statement; I'd done so with every professional that had got involved with our case over nine years. I was weary of having to go through each and every insane allegation every time a new person got involved with the case, but now with Andrew I was at ease. Karen had assured me that with his training and expertise, Andrew would make absolute sense of the details.

I believe Jane's skilful use of half-truths was transparent in her very first statement to court. Nowhere did it mention violence or an attempt to drown David; if these were true surely they would not have been missed out of a list of forty-two reasons and allegations? She now, for example, no longer repeated another insane, fabricated story of a threat to throw David over a cliff; again, surely if this were ever true she would never have stopped repeating it?

Andrew and I also spoke of why I first came to the concern that David was being abused. When David would visit me he would not go to the toilet, to the point that he would be twitching with the need but still declined when I frequently asked if he needed to go. In summer 2004, David was with me one Sunday afternoon and he began crying, exclaiming that he needed to go to the toilet. I took him to the bathroom and he sat on the toilet.

"You will have to help me clean up," David told me.

I told him that was okay, I had done that for him and my daughter when they were babies.

He then said something unusual: "This will have to be our secret, Daddy." I was distressed that David felt he could not use the toilet while in my house, but I thought no more of what he said until the next day when I told my father. He was alarmed, and told me this was not natural and cause for concern. I called the CAFCASS officer assigned to our case and she asked me to visit the offices immediately to discuss the issue. Whilst there she asked me if I thought he was being abused.

"It's never crossed my mind before, but I think it's unlikely," I replied.

"Perhaps there was something he overheard at home and misinterpreted to mean he shouldn't go to the toilet when with you," she reasoned.

That seemed logical enough for me and I gave it no further thought. However, on a subsequent phone call with Jane, I raised the issue just to discuss it. She screamed "Liar, liar!" repeatedly. This was when a kernel of concern about abuse entered my mind.

It was a difficult issue to discuss but inevitably the conversation got around to whether David was actually my son. I told Andrew I had considered a DNA test, as David not being mine was the only logical reason I could see for Jane's excessive need to deny him the love of his registered paternal family. At some point in the past I had conducted some detective work of my own. David had been born in the summer, which is always a quiet time for Jane's business. The October before, she had booked us on a weeklong holiday in the Greek Islands – in fact she had also told me that she "had calculated" it was on that holiday David had been conceived. In addition to the October break, she had also booked us a holiday that coincided with the pregnancy being two months along, which would appear in order to defer the necessary scans. When we returned home, she delayed the visit even further. When we did finally go for a scan, Jane told the nurse that we were there to determine the term so we could pitch options on a termination – something she later denied saying. It was beyond doubt that I had been outsmarted and shanghaied, and it has long been my belief that she chose me over another man because I could afford to pay child maintenance. Indeed, some time after Jane had moved out, a friend of hers told me that Jane had calculated "to the penny" how much money I would have to pay her "when" she left. But beyond all the calculations of timing, David looked like a member of my family: my friends always insisted David looked like my daughter had when she was a baby and toddler; others, including Social Services, said he was very much like me.

Regardless of that, though, what I consider to be most important is that David believes me to be his father, and I believe him to be my son. I had been there, and then fought to remain there, for his entire life, and so I wonder: How much does DNA matter?

There was good reason to doubt Jane's fidelity while we were together, though: she would delight in flirting with other men in front of me and I'd once caught her getting groped by the manager of a local hotel. I don't know why I put up with it; I reasoned that she was doing it for a reaction from me. I guess I knew I was never in love with her and as such I didn't care enough about us as a couple. I'd been willing to persevere in raising David but under the stress of the continuous presence of Jane's parents and how they would overrule me in any decisions, I'd eventually broken. I was not allowed to babysit my own son in my own home, in fact the only people allowed to look after David were Jane's parents. I thought it would eventually settle down but it actually got worse. When David was a year old I was leaving on a seven-day trip and I told Jane I had had enough, that when I returned I would have input in my son's upbringing and would no longer tolerate her father overruling me. While I was away she moved out, taking everything that we had acquired in the time we had been together. The remaining food items were out of date and the only thing left of my son's was his plastic name plate on the door to the room in which he had rarely slept. She told anyone that would listen that I had thrown them out of their home.

I explained how Jane had suggested I choose David's Christian name and shortly after doing so she stated that he would be registered with her surname, saying "We can change it after we get married." I hadn't flinched at the suggestion, but I felt manipulated: I had been allowed to choose his Christian name as a softener to justify her surname; she knew I had no intension of marrying her. The day before we registered David's birth, Jane delivered as a *fait accompli* that David's second name would be her father's Christian name. I should've raised hell but I let it go. I now sat in Andrew's office holding the opinion that I had given Jane's father the son he always wanted. Looking back on it, I could see that there was a desire to keep his maternal and paternal sides of the family separate, further evidenced by whenever I referred to my daughter Emily as David's sister, Jane and her parents would immediately jump in to say, "*Half* sister."

Andrew was very curious about Jane's father, and asked me to describe him. Before I could answer he further questioned, "Is he a big bloke?"

I hesitated before saying, "I suppose he was in his day but he's in his eighties now".

Andrew nodded and confirmed he had a mental picture of him already. Andrew also asked me about my anger at what I was being put through.

I had been expecting this question, and asked him, "Do you have a dog?" I already knew that he did, because in his office was a picture of his family and pets.

"Yes, we have two red setters."

"Do they have an aggressive temperament?" Before he could answer I continued: "Do you trust them with your children?"

Andrew did not hesitate: "Oh they are wonderful creatures, wonderful with the children. They are not an aggressive breed at all."

I nodded, and pressed on. "Put them in a corner, take a stick to them and how long do you think it will be before they growl and snarl at you?"

Andrew nodded but did not respond.

"Why is it that everyone accepts you never put yourself between an animal and its young vulnerable offspring, yet when someone blatantly positions themselves between a father and his child, if that father expresses any anger he is immediately judged as aggressive and violent? Yes, I have snarled and yes I have growled, but I have not bitten," I insisted. "I have a right to be angry, and I would consider any parent who did not show anger in the face of having their children effectively abducted from before them to be the ones in need of counselling."

Jane's tactic was to create a situation that generates a return. She then stands back and quotes the reaction as though it had been a spontaneous and unprovoked incident. I told Andrew that some years earlier Jane had taken her former employers to court for sexual harassment. "She spoke openly of this, but never once did she give an example of any harassment. The only item she told me of was a phone call after working hours from her boss who wanted her to get some information to him for an early meeting the following morning. Surely if she had been sexually harassed she would say

'So and so put his hand here or there or touched me or propositioned me'?" My interpretation of events, as I explained to Andrew, was that Jane had been moved sideways within the company or demoted to a degree, and, her ego bruised, retaliated with the allegations of sexual harassment.

When it was time for my second appointment with the psychologist, the weather had turned bitterly cold and heavy snow had fallen. As the journey was usually two hours, I decided to leave an extra hour early given the conditions. Surprisingly, all the roads were clear and I arrived an hour early. I sat in the car, with the heater on, for forty minutes, and knocked on his door twenty minutes early. This was later acknowledged in his report, with the statement: "This man wanted to be heard."

This session also lasted about four hours, and we went into a lot of detail about my family history and life as far back as I could remember. I openly discussed my relationships with my family, friends and business associates, and inevitably the subject got around to my relationships with women. I detailed the relationships I'd had that had failed for whatever reasons, the extreme guilt of the failure of my relationship with the mother of my daughter, and the delight in finally marrying Annie.

Andrew asked: "So would you say you've been unlucky in love?"

"No," I answered, "I've been extremely fortunate, but I've acted like a damn fool at times".

We discussed contact with my daughter and how it had never been an issue.

I describe my daughter's mother as a quality person; there had never been a need to go to court to establish contact. We returned to the subject of the court hearings to see David and Andrew asked why, after I had been awarded a contact order in 2000, had I not sought to progress to overnight and an annual holiday? I explained the turmoil, the heartache, re-opening old wounds and the hope that given time things would mellow; I expressed my disgust and lack of faith in the Family Court process and the cost of legal services. I also relayed that I had tried to broach the subject with Jane at which she had venomously delivered: "If you get overnight contact I will take him (David) a long, long way away" in a manner that I took to suggest she regarded me as a pervert. I shrugged my shoulders, "Perhaps I should've persevered at the time but I chose not to" and considered myself to be damned whatever I do. "Jane refused to grant me the right to parental responsibility on the grounds that I didn't know what drugs David was allergic to. The judge at the time asked me if this was correct. 'It has not been established that David is allergic to any drugs,' I had responded, and Jane then maintained I was wrong. The judge turned to Jane and asked her for the name of the drugs he was allergic to. Jane named only one, Erythromycin. The judge wrote the name down on a piece of paper, handed it to me, and declared, 'There, Mr Moore now knows the name of the drug. Are you happy for me to now award him parental responsibility?' Jane of course refused, but the judge awarded it anyway. The thing is Andrew, it is Jane, not David, who is allergic to Erythromycin, but she thinks because she's allergic to it, David must be also."

By the time the appointment was over I was mentally drained, but I had homework as well. Andrew gave me two lists of multiple-choice questions to complete, totalling almost seven hundred. I completed them the next day. The instructions Andrew had given me were to answer them as quickly and honestly as possible and not dwell on anything, which was not so easy. Obviously the questions were structured purposely and I found myself honestly answering a question only to find my answer to the following question would contradict the previous answer. They were simple enough to complete, but when I'd finished I felt I'd screwed the whole damn thing up.

For my part, I had driven the two-hour journey to Andrew's office for the meetings, but Jane had not been so accommodating. She had refused to visit him, so Andrew had to go and see Jane according to her schedule.

My daughter, Emily, had settled with her partner Paul in New Zealand. He had found employment quickly, and she was happy to be a waitress while sorting out visas and finding work in real estate. Annie and I had planned a trip to see them, and our tickets had been booked for close to a year. Everyone involved in proceedings knew our schedule.

Social Services had asked us to make a couple of video diaries to show David when we got back. We obliged, and took one while sailing and the other from the top of Langkawi Island's Sky Bridge, 125 metres up a mountain overlooking the ocean. I told the camera what fun we were having, and said, "One day I'll bring you here son." Our flight from there took us to New Zealand, and by coincidence it was the same plane as the UK rugby team, which meant we had a spectacular Haka welcome at the airport.

We stayed with my daughter and her fiancé for a few days before renting a car and driving for many miles, taking in the sights. They joined us in Queenstown on the third week of our trip and we took a few more videos for David, featuring his sister too. We left the car there and the four of us flew back to Emily and Paul's in the North Island. Because their home was small, Emily had found us a great deal with a hotel owned by her friends. As we checked in I logged onto the Internet and heard that Jane's father had collapsed and been rushed to hospital. A subsequent email announced that he had died.

I cannot say I was upset at the news. He had helped create the difficult situation over the years, and while both my parents had died without being allowed access to David, he had passed away just as the tide was turning. Not only did he have the pleasure of his grandchild, but David had his name too! My only concern was David's emotions at his death.

I recalled how a member of Jane's extended family had once told me, "You don't stand a chance until the old man is in a box." That day had come, although in some ways I regretted not being able to get even with him. I found this to be a frequent problem throughout my struggle: sometimes you lose sight of the target. The main objective is of course the child, but you can be so emotionally distraught that you lose focus and get distracted in fighting the system. Thankfully, Karen had covered these situations with me and whenever I found myself seeking a counter-score I quickly recognised that I needed to stop. This was something I had learned over and over again at the education classes with CSF.

When we returned from our trip, Tina went on maternity leave and a new caseworker, Elizabeth, was assigned. Naturally, we had concerns at the idea of yet another new person coming to the case and the worry that it would set us back again. There was no need to fret, though; the new caseworker was fully briefed and just as assertive as Tina.

On March 15, we were back in court. The psychologist and paediatrician's reports on David's health issues were completed, both of which exceeded eighty pages. Social Services had been analysing the reports for some days, but they only became available to the other parties twenty-four hours before court. James, from Social Services, had continued to establish a bond of trust with David and updated us along the way with reports on how he was and how our holiday videos had been received.

Prior to the hearing, I was summoned to a meeting at Jane's solicitor's office. Also in attendance were members of the Social Services personnel, David's legal guardian and solicitor, and an abundance of tea, sandwiches and biscuits. I thought it strange to be meeting like this, and as I entered the room and saw Jane was absent I realised something major was about to happen.

With the pleasantries done, the Social Services team leader took me into a vacant room and wasted no words: "We are taking David into care."

The words hit me like a brick and tears welled in my eyes. I felt an immense surge of conflicting emotions: there was the relief that after all we had endured something was finally going to be done, but also apprehension of what David would be going through as he was taken into care. I couldn't talk without my voice cracking, but I asked for reassurances from Social Services that they had everything covered with a suitable foster family.

I was politely cut off mid-sentence as my questions had already been anticipated, and I was assured of what David's experiences would be for each coming step. I was also given an apology for Social Services not heeding my previous warnings and failing David earlier, but the team was now totally on track. With my tears subsided and my voice returned, we went back to the main office to join the others.

It was clear that everyone knew what I had just been told. Jane's solicitor offered words of satisfaction that the process was moving forward, then turned to me and said he believed we both shared the same opinion of Jane's father. I remained silent; my opinion of the solicitor was still that he lacked emotion and profited from the abuse of my son, and his statement did not change that. I have always agreed that Jane was entitled to legal representation, but in my eyes this man helped her navigate the Family Law process and as a result had effectively assisted in the abuse of my son.

David's solicitor asked a number of questions, and discussions went back and forth between the professionals as I sat quietly in a hollow zone, listening to echoes of what was being said around me. David's solicitor then told me that as of now I would require legal representation. Wanting to avoid small town local solicitors, as most had at some time been employed by Jane, I asked Adam Davies if he knew of anyone.

"Sorry Thomas, but for ethical reasons I cannot make recommendations," he replied.

I smiled. "It is important that whoever I have representing me can get along with you. It doesn't have to be a recommendation."

After repeated disclaimers of him not being able to make recommendations, I decided to search the web for a suitable firm in the city. We left the meeting and walked to the court, and I phoned Annie and Karen en-route with the update.

When we entered the court, Jane was in the waiting room with a female friend.

In the court hearing with Judge Renhold, Social Services made it clear they wanted to take David into care. Jane's solicitor requested an application to adjourn, but this was refused.

Judge Renhold discussed that Judge Marks reside on the care hearing and talks began for an immediate start the next day. Social Services advised for Andrew Green, the psychologist, to be called as a witness.

There were concerns regarding David being kept safe in the meantime and being kept ignorant of what was going to happen in court over the next few days – it was well known that he had been made to know everything from a very early age. So it was agreed that Jane's friend, who was still in the waiting area, would be in charge of David's security by staying with Jane and David for the next few days. Her duties would include checking that David was not informed of what was happening in court and that he remained safe. On that, the hearing ended and we all left to mull over the week ahead.

I called a number from my internet search results and was soon talking to a female solicitor. Her name was Rebecca and she was on the train following another hearing. I gave her a brief overview of the situation and advised Adam Davies was acting on behalf of my son.

"I can get the relevant files emailed to me and be in court fully briefed tomorrow," she said.

I was impressed, not only with her obvious work ethic but her demeanour in general: she was polite, articulate, sharp as a knife and, being from the city, it was clear she had handled cases like this before. Her confidence was so strong it practically oozed out of my phone, and the image in my mind was of a Mary Poppins character in stilettos – a strong, caring, determined, confident and successful woman. This woman knew how to get the job done, of that there was no doubt.

CHAPTER 16

On the following day, March 16, I was in the court's waiting area when the professionals arrived in their respective groups. Jane was there with her friend again, who had now signed to confirm she would stay with Jane to look after David.

A lady in her mid to late thirties entered and started to scan the room for a face to acknowledge her. I smiled and nodded, presuming it was Rebecca.

"Thomas, I'm Rebecca," she said with a handshake. "Good to meet you. Let's get some privacy to talk this over."

Obligingly, I followed her and we went into a separate room for discussions. She had certainly done her homework, and advised me on what was likely to happen in the coming days. I was easily lost in the legal terminology and the maze of possible scenarios I was presented with, but suffice to say, Adam Davies was correct: I did need legal representation and I had faith that Rebecca was the right person for the job.

I figured on our first meeting I would need to discuss her fees and expenses. I was well acquainted with legal representation costs from the proceeding ten years and, considering inflation and her being from the city, Rebecca would not operate at bargain basement prices. I had chosen not to discuss fees on the phone, reasoning that at this point in proceedings they would have to be paid regardless. I braced myself for impact and broached the subject.

"Oh, it's all paid for," she replied, explaining that because these were Social Services proceedings, and all parties should therefore receive representation, "Legal Aid covers the costs."

On learning that my bank account would not be drained by these hearings, I offered to buy the coffees – at just thirty pence a cup from the vending machine, I was more than happy to cover the costs!

The hearing opened with the barrister for Social Services explaining the case and the need for David to be taken into care. Following that, the Social Services administrator of the team that had been working with David was called to give evidence. She gave a comprehensive breakdown of events since Social Services had been instructed to conduct a Section 37 report. Questions were asked by everyone except my own brief because, as Rebecca later explained, all points that were our concern had been covered. A woman named Tanya Long had been instated as David's new legal guardian; she was present on the sidelines and liaising with Social Services about David's progress.

Next up was the Social Services manager, who again covered the Section 37 report and outlined the care plan for David. Social Services had said that CAMHS (Child and Adolescent Mental Health Services)[2] would get involved and was willing to work with "the family" once David was in a permanent placement. CAMHS believed

---

[2] CAMHS is part of the National Health Service and works to help young people and their families. CAMHS specialises in providing help and treatment for children and young people with emotional, behavioural and mental health difficulties. (Information taken from the CAMHS website.)

it would be wrong for David to have direct counselling because it would make him believe that he was in the wrong. Instead, CAMHS suggested that its members would work with the family of David's permanent home to help them handle him through the transition and help him come to understand what had occurred in his life. Social Services also stated that they had the means, i.e. the infrastructure and budget, to take care of David for "as long as it takes," and emphasised that he could be kept with a permanent foster family until he came of age. It would be this permanent foster family that would liaise with CAMHS.

"Why has it taken so long for Social Services to get involved?" Judge Marks asked the manager.

"There have been many missed opportunities," she replied.

She worded that differently to yesterday, I thought, *when she told me the system had failed.*

The process moved a lot slower than I had expected, although that was most likely because I had only seen court scenes in film dramas. There was much of what I felt to be condescending and smarmy statements from all the professionals to Judge Marks. "Thank you for your time sir," "May I respectfully request sir," and so on. I would describe Marks as a portly sixty-something gentleman whose body language and demeanour I interpret to be worthy of his position, a fair and unbiased man only interested in facts. He demonstrated himself to be a wise old owl.

The paediatrician had completed an extensive study of David's health issues dating back to when he was born. Over the years I had made comments and notes on my office wall calendar each time there had been a cancelled contact session. It was these calendars and the school absence reports that Karen had worked so fastidiously with in her analysis and now, with the benefit of David's doctor's file, every individual issue had been scrutinised and held to account in detail.

Jane had often passed comment when cancelling a contact that David had seen the doctor or nurse or been to A&E, or sometimes she said she had just been to the chemist with him, and now her tactic had become illustrated. Jane had alternated between various medical advice and services with David in a manner that could not be easily cross-referenced. The study showed the pattern I had raised concern about around travel schedules. It showed attendances of doctor's appointments and A&E visits far in excess of the norm and usually for very minor ailments. It also displayed an alarming pattern of health issues around the schedule of legal proceedings. For example, contact had been cancelled with the explanation that David was on antibiotics after Jane had taken him to the doctor because of a slight rash on his arm. It had only required a cream, and was not something that could justify cancelling contact, but she had the ammunition that he had been to the doctor's and was now on antibiotics. It was yet another blatant manipulation of the truth.

As I had anticipated, the report did not unveil any evidence of Jane inducing illness in David, but how could an investigation five years after the event be conclusive? I doubt an investigation twenty-four hours after I had predicated David's illnesses would have unearthed anything out of the ordinary, given how easy it is to induce vomiting using simple products found around the average home. This made reading of the eighty-page report difficult, as I began to think it would conclude that Jane had done nothing wrong – but the last page nailed it. In the absence of any evidence that she induced illness in David, Jane was diagnosed as being at "the far end of Munchhausen by Proxy" in that she had manipulated David's health issues in a manner to suit her agenda.

Andrew's report had been equally lengthy and contained a thorough character analysis of Jane, David and myself. I was disappointed to read some of what I had discussed, as at the time I believed certain information was personal and, although I deemed it pertinent for Andrew to hear, I did not believe it required mention in the report for all to see.

I was assessed as having certain character traits, failings, strengths and weaknesses. It detailed my frustrations and various issues, but nothing beyond the norm and nothing that presented me as a threat to society or lacking ability to be a parent.

Jane's profile received a similar measure of analysis and in the field of her family history Andrew reported her parents and her life to date as being described by Jane as "perfect". Andrew followed this with the observation that during the entire interview and Jane's relaying of her childhood not once did she mention her sister, so he did not therefore believe things could have been as wonderful as she described them to be. Andrew described Jane as being a highly manipulative woman who takes liberties with the truth, and a woman who seeks to devolve responsibility for problems of her own making onto others. She was also measured as "off the scale" on narcissism, and David shared many of Jane's traits to an alarming degree.

The second day hearing, on March 17, started with the psychologist Andrew Green being called as a witness. He was questioned by the Social Services barrister and David's solicitor. Neither Rebecca nor Jane's brief asked anything. The questions were determining the emotional harm David had been subjected to, and explored the possibilities of him being able to adjust to a new situation away from the present enmeshment he had with his mother.

"I can confirm that David has clearly suffered emotional harm, but I cannot offer any guarantees of success should he be put into care," Andrew said. "However, I must emphasise that to leave him where he is now will certainly cause more harm. It is my opinion that David will benefit from direct counselling in a one-to-one setting to help him come to terms with the situation." He also confirmed that I had done everything possible to establish and maintain a relationship with my son, but that Jane had "gone to extreme lengths to erase the entire paternal family from David's life."

Judge Marks then asked, "What of the Jesuit maxim, give me a child for his first seven years and I'll give you the man?"

Andrew's posture was held firm and exuded confidence in the witness box. He maintained eye contact with the judge as he spoke: "There are no guarantees of success, sir."

Jane was next into the witness box; it was strange to see her holding a bible and swearing to tell the truth, the whole truth and nothing but.

The Social Services barrister started questioning. He began with asking her to outline various dates and timespans, and Jane struggled to recall how long it had been since I last saw David. She stammered and then looked in my direction. I kept my elbow on the desk and raised four fingers, one for each year that I had not seen him. Jane then confirmed four years. Various other dates pertaining to David's school attendance records were established, and Jane agreed. She began to ramble that she was everything to David and he would be torn apart without her, as well that now her father had died, she realised the importance of a father figure.

A raised hand from the barrister silenced her and he altered his posture from a forward lean to now standing upright, shoulders back and chin up. When he started I thought he was a condescending wimp, but he underwent a transformation. He became someone not to mess with and who demanded respect. He quoted David's schedule of health problems, which tied in directly with the schedule of events Jane had previously agreed were correct.

"Do you accept the pattern of your son's illnesses fits this schedule?" he asked.

Jane stuttered and struggled for words. "Yes, but it is a coincidence," she tried.

"No. Do you accept you are responsible for making your son ill?" he demanded.

Jane was in such a mess I actually felt sorry for her. The barrister raised his voice a notch. I could now understand why Social Services had chosen him as representation. He repeated the question.

Jane struggled for words again and, with tears in her eyes, she meekly said, "I suppose it might look like that."

The barrister repeated the question again, this time his voice booming.

"If I did it was not intentional," came the submissive reply.

The judge ordered a break and private discussions with the legal representatives. I left the courtroom to use the bathroom, and on my way back I passed Jane's friend in the waiting area. She glanced at me and I walked over to her side of the room. Without looking at her, I said as I walked past, "Thank you for everything you are doing for David. I am very grateful." I did not wait for a reply, and carried on to the hall leading to the courtroom. As I was talking to Rebecca, the Social Services barrister walked past me and, with a lowered voice, said: "You are the only one in here who will come out of this smelling of roses." With that, he continued on his way.

I looked at Rebecca. "What was that about?"

"He's right," she replied.

Right or not, I couldn't dwell on the comment; my concerns were what lay ahead for David.

The legal parties all went into the judge's chambers at the back of the courtroom and the rest of us were free to walk around and talk amongst ourselves. I knew that if David was ordered into care it was planned to happen without Jane getting to see him. It was now late afternoon and David would be on his way to Jane's mother's house from school, escorted by a social worker.

After some time, the legal teams emerged from the chamber. The Social Services barrister went to the corridor to reception where the Social Services team had congregated, and I noticed the boss and barrister looked at one another. The barrister nodded at her. The boss turned to one of the Social Services staff, shared eye contact and a nod, then the member of staff left. I realised David was about to be taken into care.

We took our seats again. The judge took his time re-entering the room, and when he did we all stood. I was unable to control my emotions; the tears began swelling in my eyes as I saw the nods between the Social Services team, and as the judge began to explain that David would be taken into care, I wept. I had no tissues, and had to resort to wiping my tears away with my hands and sleeves like a schoolboy, but I did not care.

Jane sat stone-faced with zero emotion.

I cannot express the sorrow, pain and fear I held for what our son was about to experience.

After Judge Marks made his announcement, we left the courtroom. Jane remained emotionless as her solicitor led her into a private room off reception, her friend in tow. Seconds later she began screaming and crying, to my ears it sounded theatrical.

We had been ordered to return to court the following day, March 18, for the judge's summing up. The Social Services boss took me aside. "Mr Moore, I must assure you again that David will be perfectly safe. All sensitivity is being applied. The family David will be living with are wonderful people, and he will be attending his usual school as normal. Would you like the address and phone number of the family?" she asked.

I declined. I cannot explain why, other than it was not something I had previously thought of and the impact had been so immense that at that moment I felt it was inconsequential to know where he was. I had not seen him in four years, so as long as I knew he was with good people I was satisfied. "Could you please give them my number instead, and ask them to call me if and when they feel the time is right?" They had their work cut out for them and I did not want them to have any extra pressure from me.

I left court and phoned Annie and Karen. Then I wandered home and spent the night in a state of sorrow and astonishment. As I went to bed, I wondered how David was feeling, in a strange new home and bed.

The next morning I was greeted at court by the Social Services boss, who updated me on what had happened after David had been taken into care. She had moments before received a call from James, the Family Support worker David had an established relationship with and who had driven him to school that morning. James himself had been taken into care when he was eleven years old and he shared that with David in the car. The revelation was something David took comfort from, and James reported that David was upbeat, even singing in the car.

In the courtroom the judge read his ruling. It took a long time because he was articulate and referred to every aspect of the experts' concerns. The ruling expressed deep anxiety for David and condemned Jane's parenting. He repeated the psychologist's remark that I had done everything I possibly could.

I had waited many, many years, and David and my family had gone through hell. Yet I did not feel any satisfaction in being vindicated. My son had been taken into care, and my emotions lay firmly in yearning for his peace of mind.

CHAPTER 17

On March 24 Annie and I received a letter from David's school in which the headmaster felt we should all know about David's progress. Apparently he was upbeat and handling things very positively.

We had an appointment for the two social workers assigned to our case to visit home and go through a required session on parenting. We spent around an hour and a half drinking tea, eating biscuits and flipping prompt cards with assorted scenarios of parent/child situations. Annie and I were required to share our opinions and observations on whatever subject came up, and given that we both had children older than these social workers it was amusing to everyone. There were numerous instances where the generation gap was all too apparent, but we had no worries and all was fine.

Since getting involved with David, the Family Support programme had worked on several exercises with him, one of which was a family history, covering who he was and who was in his family, all backed up with photos and discussions of good times with everyone. Sadly, on the occasions when I had been mentioned, David had always referred to me by my Christian name and not expressed any wish to see me.

James, the Family Support worker, was giving us daily updates on David's progress and what he was doing. I was already aware from local newspaper articles that David was keen on a couple of sports activities, and James had been building a rapport with him visiting the local golf driving range and the sports centre for table tennis. The plan was that when he felt able to, David would write me a letter and challenge me to a game.

On one occasion when Annie and I were driving home from a stay with her brother and his fiancée, my phone rang. Annie answered because I was driving; it was David's foster mother calling to introduce herself and report on how he was doing. I pulled over into a lay-by and took the call. Her voice was that of a younger woman, but she explained that she was an experienced mother with her own children and one other teenage fostered child. She reported David to be doing fine although she was originally concerned that Social Services had made the correct placement.

"David is very quiet and ours is a mad house," she explained.

I was halfway between tears and laughter as I reassured her that was exactly what David needed – to experience a real family.

"He is also very polite, to the point of extreme. For example, once he had his breakfast cereal put in front of him, he would wait and ask, 'Can I start?' I also asked David why he did not want to see you, and he replied with words to the effect that you had been unkind to him. I told him we all make mistakes and people deserve second chances."

This gentle encouragement for David to warm to his father was touching, and I appreciated what she was trying to do.

We spoke for a while longer and agreed that she and her husband would meet me the following Tuesday evening at a local pub close to where David would be attending the sports centre.

When the following Tuesday rolled around, I arrived at the pub as agreed. As I entered the building I saw a couple keenly observing who was coming in. I smiled and they smiled back – I had introduced myself to my son's foster parents, Dana and Jeff. I ordered a coffee, and was so nervous I needed two hands to hold the cup steady. They are a good few years younger than me, as I had anticipated from the phone call, but they were not short of parenting experience and both were very personable. Dana was dressed immaculately and fashionably, and Jeff had greeted me with a firm handshake and looked me straight in the eye – qualities that I took to show he was a man with a strong personality, a trait I was happy my son's foster dad exhibited.

We spoke about David and what had happened in our lives for him to be taken into care, and I was pleased to see that they had been fully briefed by Social Services.

"I must admit to still being concerned that perhaps David would be better placed in a quieter family," Dana said.

"Please be assured, the full normal environment is ideal for him," I explained. This was something I had discussed with Karen Woodall, and she had agreed with me.

The three of us spoke for about an hour, and in that time I had two coffees. Dana and Jeff not only spoke very caringly about David, but they also asked me many questions to glean as much information about him as possible. I was only too happy to oblige.

All too soon they had to leave to collect David from the sports centre, so we said our goodbyes and agreed to speak on the phone regarding progress towards reintroducing me into David's life.

A few days later the Family Support worker gave me a note from David:

Dad, I will be playing James (FSW) at table tennis tomorrow at 1 o'clock if you come I will beat you, David.

It was lovely but strange to read. I assumed he had been prompted to write it and it was concise, to say the least, but at last my son was inviting me to meet.

The following day, Annie and I walked to the sports centre. The reception staff directed us to the rear of the building, where a large room had a full-size table tennis table. We could hear the *ping, pong* sounds of play in progress and recognised the voices of James and David. As I entered the room, I did my best to subdue my delight in seeing my son so much taller and grown up since I had last seen him. We sat down while they finished their game, making some fun comments and trying to keep score. Eventually I was invited to play, and I was easily dispatched. We all had a turn and made conversation about the game. At one point James announced that he was going to the vending machine in the lobby to get drinks, and David was happy to be left alone with Annie and I. This was noted in a later report.

I had always maintained that my son would have no genuine recollection of any harm he had come to while with either myself or Annie, simply because there had never been such a time; rather, the thoughts had just been hammered into him by his mother and maternal grandparents. It therefore stood to reason that by spending real time with me, he would overcome those false recollections.

We stayed for around forty-five minutes and all left together. Annie and I walked home, while James and David drove back to Dana and Jeff's.

Finally, I had spent some quality time with my son.

CHAPTER 18

On April 6, 2010, Annie and I signed a parenting agreement at the request of Social Services. The agreement had us promise to adhere to criteria, such as not discussing proceedings with David or talking negatively about Jane or her family. A short while after signing it we again met David and James, this time at the golf driving range. It was a fun day and it had been agreed that James would make excuses to leave early, with Annie and I taking David back to his foster home.

As chance would have it, one of Jane's distant relations happened to also be at the driving range that day. She had always made it known to me that she disagreed with how Jane was treating David and she was pleased that we were together now. She was aware of Social Services being involved and what was going on. Over the years though I had taken very little comfort in any support I was given by anyone involved with Jane; I felt that if they thought David was being subjected to injustice they should tell Jane so, not merely tell me how sad it is.

Since he had been taken into care David had been ferried to and from school, which was a sixteen-mile round trip, by either James, other members of Social Services, or a private taxi. Dana and Jeff proved to be wonderful, making sure he was included in their family activities. Jane was allowed contact only via letters that were subject to being edited and censored by Social Services if necessary; David was free to write to her anytime he wanted, and had started off doing so everyday but that gradually decreased to being rather infrequent. Annie and I were solely included more in contact until it was finally arranged that I would be able to collect David in the mornings, drop him off at school, pick him up in the afternoon and take him back to his foster home again.

On April 15, Social Services held a meeting and agreed that David would be removed from the Child Protection Plan as he was no longer in the environment he was in when it was concluded that he was at risk of harm from his mother. David's foster parents were also at the meeting and gave a full report of his progress – he was doing well, but he frequently needed the toilet. The social worker who had collected David from his grandmother's house when he had been ordered into care had completed a statement of the event in neat handwriting. It stated that Jane's mother had repeatedly said, "You cannot do this to me" and continually said that she had recently lost her husband and other reasons why David could not be taken away. It was reported that she did not express any concern for David at the time, and that David had been supportive, reassuring his grandmother that everything would be fine. The social worker's report praised his maturity as a result of that. In addition to that report, several of Jane's friends had written letters to Social Services bosses and the local MP criticising the actions of Social Services, and these were read out in the meeting. The MP had gone on to write to Social Services on the matter, diplomatically enquiring about their actions.

This inspired me to write to the MP to request an appointment to discuss my version of events. I contacted him through his website and received an almost immediate phone call from his secretary, wanting to know when I was available.

"Anytime," I replied.

Within hours I was at the MP's office, giving a brief history of matters and reminding him that, contrary to the claims in the letters he received, Social Services had not simply taken David into care. It had been a decision made by a judge after hearing many hours of evidence from many professionals. I also explained that Social Services had tried, over many months, to work with Jane but with no success. "If there should be any questions raised about Social Services and their actions, it should be focused on their lack of action when I had alerted them in 2006," I declared, before commending the team currently working with David. I also discussed Karen Woodall and the Centre for Separated Families: "Were it not for Karen's work, it is most likely that nothing would have been done. Yet despite this, government funding to the centre is being cut."

At that comment he raised an eyebrow and asked me to repeat Karen's name and the CSF address. We discussed the political nature of Family Law and I asked: "Why does the government repeatedly talk about broken families when there are hundreds if not thousands of children being denied the love of their parents, essentially being abducted from half of their relatives?"

The MP was receptive to hearing my side of events, although I expected nothing other than having him understand there was more to the case than what Jane's friends believed.

I do not know if it was a coincidence or not, and I will never know for sure, but Karen later informed me that the Centre for Separated Families had been awarded new government funding.

By now David was used to stopping at our home for tea on the way home from school before I took him back to Dana and Jeff's. My daughter Emily was delighted to have her little brother back in her life, having spoken to him on the phone and Skype by now. It wasn't too much longer until the professionals decided that the time was right to suggest to David that he should stay over one night while his foster parents were "busy". I was ecstatic that he was fine with the idea, and he stayed over one night later that week. A few days earlier I had found a full-size table tennis table on eBay and it arrived the same day he was spending the night. This meant we were able to spend some time together assembling it in the loft over the garage, then spend more quality time together by playing a few games. I didn't know it when I ordered it, but that table transpired to be an excellent tool for communication for us.

When the time came for David to go to bed he asked me if he could read for a while. I agreed. He told me that the door needed to be left open at a precise angle and the landing light also needed to be left on all night. He had brought with him a picture of Jane and a lavender spray, both of which were put on the bedside table. As I hugged him goodnight he asked for the spray and squirted lavender four times onto each of the three pillows. "This helps me sleep," he explained.

When I went to leave the room he was concerned that I would move the door, and asked me to check on him every five minutes. I countered with every fifteen minutes and we then agreed on ten. I went back upstairs three times: the first was to make sure he had finished reading and turned his light off, the second was to reassure him I was still there and checking on him as requested, and the third time was to see if he had fallen asleep.

In the morning I woke him up for school and he was in good spirits. When I picked him up from school later that afternoon I returned him to his foster parents. The overnight stay had been a success and the following week he stayed over for two nights, each time with the same bedtime routine.

Jeff had bought David a BMX and he had started to learn to ride it. It found its way to my home and it thrilled me to be part of my son learning to ride his bike for the first time.

On May 22 Annie and I were due to go away on a cruise around the Norwegian Fjords with some American friends. The trip had been booked for a year but shortly before it began a volcanic eruption in Iceland made air travel problematic, therefore our American friends had to cancel. Annie and I were still planning on taking the trip though, and the schedule was on the agenda with Social Services progress arrangements. I was torn between wanting to progress as fast as possible with David and also look after Annie – she had supported me (and continues to) one hundred per cent at all times and I was looking forward to spending quality time together and taking the opportunity to spoil her.

With us being booked to be away it had been decided for David to stay two nights during the week, and other than his bedtime routine all went smoothly, so we decided to extend it another night. The last morning together was Thursday and we were due to leave on Saturday. I collected David from school with the plan that he would stay for tea before I took him back to Dana and Jeff's. However, in the afternoon while David was with us I got a call from the Social Services case worker who asked if she could visit "urgently". I agreed and she asked if we could talk outside of earshot of David. "Yes, I can work in the garage and leave David playing upstairs with Annie supervising," I replied, very concerned with how official it sounded and as though something was wrong.

"How is David doing?" she asked when she arrived.

"Great," I replied.

"We've got a problem with his placement," she said, and both her tone and manner were not the casual rapport we had established. "Don't worry, David is not, and has not been, at any risk of harm, but he will need to be relocated and won't be returned to Dana and Jeff's tonight."

"But he's doing great with us, I can't see how moving him to another family at this time will be a positive move. Could he not stay with us?" I reasoned.

"That is most likely to be agreed to by my superiors, provided David is happy with it," she said.

We walked into the house and she sensitively discussed it with David. He did not hesitate in agreeing to stay with Annie and myself.

"Are Dana and Jeff okay?" I asked.

"I'm sorry, but I cannot say any more than David has never been at risk of harm but he cannot stay there any longer," she replied.

"You are aware of our trip on Saturday, would it be possible to get David's passport and book him to join us on the trip?" I enquired.

"I'll look into it and let you know."

The following day I took David to school and then called the travel agents to discuss the possibility of getting David on the cruise. There were phone calls to make and I was told they would call me back later that day – less than twenty-four hours before the ship was setting sail.

Social Services called me mid-morning and confirmed that David could stay with us, but there were some questions on getting hold of his passport. By mid-afternoon it had been confirmed that we would not be able to get his passport in time, and when the travel agent called back I informed him that I would have to cancel the trip. Insurance did not cover such cancellations. I had no qualms about losing the money – my only concerns were that both my son and my wife were happy. Annie, as ever, was understanding and supportive. Each of these incidents has reaffirmed how blessed I am to have her.

When David returned from school that afternoon, he was walking into his new home – with his father.

CHAPTER 19

I received a call from Jeff in May, a short while after David had moved in with us permanently. Jeff was distraught and explained that the family had been accused of something that he described as "outrageous" by someone close to them. I had liked Jeff from the moment we had met and he and Dana had helped bring about a change in David's life that I will forever remain grateful for. They were both beside themselves with grief, not just because of the situation with their daughter and losing David, but because they were going to have to now face a review by the county council. I had total empathy for them and I was determined to support them in whatever way I could. I assured them that they would continue to play a significant role in David's life. He had established an important bond with them and I saw them as posing no risk to him at all; they were a very positive influence.

Later that same day I received a call from Jane.

"What have they done to him? My god is he alright?" she asked forcefully. She had been told the same thing I had, and I told her that David was absolutely fine and had never been at risk. Jane still had her tendency to twist details to suit her own interests, evidenced by the fact that months later I was in the company of one of her girlfriends who said, "Yes, David came to live with you after the foster family abused him." I corrected her on that and several other issues that she mentioned, not least the paradox of false accusations, firstly preventing me from seeing my son to them now ensuring he live with me.

Annie and I were in a strange situation of effectively fostering my own son. We were picking up the bills for David while in a void of sharing parental responsibility with Social Services. James became like an addition to the family, often calling into our home to demolish chocolate cake and truckers-sized mugs of tea. I had to admire and respect the role he had established in David's life – the slip of a lad I had been so cynical of on our first meeting proved himself to be anything but!

"Have you applied for the Child Benefit to be transferred to you?" James asked me.

I hadn't even given it a thought. I made the application online that day and received a call a few days later from the Benefit Office, asking me to confirm my details and provide further information. I was frustrated and surprised to learn than Jane was entitled to receive, and continued to receive, the Child Benefit despite David being taken from her over two months earlier. On establishing with the Benefit Office that David was now living with us, I was advised that Jane had "kindly agreed" to us receiving the benefits two weeks before she was legally obliged to stop receiving them. I decided to question the caller.

"So, you abuse your child, all the while subsidised by Legal Aid, then when the child is taken into care you can still keep claiming Child Benefits?"

I was given an explanation of the rules under which Child Benefits are awarded.

"Do you not look at the taxes you pay from your salary and wonder what the hell we are doing?"

She diplomatically confirmed that she did.

In early June Social Services held a Looked After Child (LAC) Review, which was attended by all the professionals involved with David, Annie, myself, Jane and a male friend she referred to as her supporter. It did not escape my attention that it was the same person who had appeared from nowhere when I had anticipated David would be ill at Christmas 2005, and Jane was trying to wash vomit from the car door.

It was half term and David's headmaster, who had been extremely supportive throughout the process, went out of his way to attend the review. It began with Jane's supporter giving a bigoted, misguided verbal lashing towards the Social Services staff, and I was amazed that they said nothing to defend their actions or correct him. He claimed that they had torn a family apart.

With the Social Services remaining silent, I took it upon myself to respond. "Far from tearing a family apart, Social Services have united a family. You are clearly not aware of all the facts."

My statement made no impact whatsoever, and he tore into the headmaster next, deriding the letter he had written shortly after David had been taken into care.

This annoyed the headmaster. He sat upright, red in the face, and in an assertive tone enquired: "What qualification do you have, sir, in the area of child development?"

Jane's supporter was silent for a moment, then said: "I've witnessed David at a barbeque, happy with his mother."

The headmaster repeated the question, and received a reply as wet as the original but extended to further scorn the school letter.

"Are you questioning the integrity of my staff, sir?" the headmaster boomed.

There was a reply even more timid than the first, running along the same lines as the initial accusation.

The headmaster was so infuriated he was trembling and he repeated his question in a demanding tone.

Jane's supporter stayed silent. He had made a total fool of himself to the entire room, but he and Jane sat down with an air of superiority. Jane had deliberately refrained from correcting her supporter on issues that she was fully aware he was wrong, and it became obvious that she had supplied him with incorrect information. What she had failed to realise was that she had demonstrated total denial and had, as a result, set back progress to restoring contact between herself and David. Sitting there then, I remembered how I had also defended Jane based on only the information she had given me. I was still awestruck by her ability to manipulate anyone around her, and it did not escape my knowledge that I had been the biggest fool of all.

The meeting ended shambolically, but Social Services were happy that David was being looked after safely and that contact with his mother and maternal grandmother would be supervised at all times.

It was also around this time that we heard that Jane had fallen out with the friend who had attended court with her and agreed to oversee David during the hearing that ordered him into care. Our thoughts were that in going to court with Jane she had been given a deeper insight into the situation and she didn't like what she saw. During this same period of time, Jane began a relationship with a man named Graham, whose mother was a close friend of Jane's mother.

The legalities of proceedings may not have been as tidy as I would have liked, but David and I were bonding quickly and putting the table tennis table to great use. We had improved our game, discussed a lot of things about his life and shared many emotional times in the loft of the garage as we played. We had also managed to get David past his obsessive insecurity of his bedtime routine of the lavender spray, specific door angle and frequent checks from me.

David naturally wanted to know why he had to be taken away from his mother, and I was in the impossible situation of having to reassure him without talking negatively about his mother or her parents. There were several nights when the emotional outpouring extended to bedtime and there were occasions when I held him tightly as he sobbed and doubted whether the removal from his mother was in fact for the best. At times like this, Karen became a rock for me to lean on alongside Annie. Karen was an oracle to me, and her voice alone was enough to reassure me. She had the experience and ability to explain in simple terms what David was going through and what his exact needs were at any given time. Doubting and questioning your actions is healthy, and Karen always assured me that we were on the correct course for the ultimate best interest of David's development. The best thing for me though was I knew she had no hesitation in telling me if I was doing something wrong.

Annie became aware that Jane had contacted her ex-husband to try to get details on why they split up.

Annie's ex knew Jane was somewhat off the wall, and he told Annie that Jane was trying to find some dirt so she could discredit Annie and, by default, me. Our initial emotion was to be infuriated, but Karen explained that this was to be expected of Jane and that it ultimately would work against her in illustrating her denial.

"Where are the original accusations now? If they were true she would not have dropped them, instead of looking to dig up dirt she should be addressing her own problems. Don't worry, this all works for you and against her," Karen explained.

Annie and I began attending CAMHS appointments about every six weeks. It was frustrating that it was Jane in need of help but because the court could not order her to get it, it was our responsibility to learn how to help David come to terms with his mother's behaviour. The irony was that some years before I had been driving an eighty-mile round trip to attend classes that helped me come to terms with David's behaviour, such as his eating scrambled egg in a restaurant with his fingers at the age of six, and Jane had told everyone I was in anger management classes. Now that Annie and I were having to learn how to help David handle his mother's personality disorder, Jane was telling people that we were in need of help from CAMHS even though we had been given custody of David. Sometimes it felt like banging your head against a brick wall, because no matter what we did or why we did it, it was twisted to suit her stance.

CAMHS assigned us two Adolescent Mental Health Workers; both had been briefed on Jane's behavioural pattern and David's situation in now living with us. On occasion I felt as though I had used the meetings to vent my frustrations rather than address David's issues directly, although at the same time I suppose that the two are interlinked – if I could get my frustrations out I could have a better mind-set from which to be a better parent to David. I was able to take from most visits constructive ideas on tackling his traits and we were also given a lot of insight into what he would be going through and how his perceptions would be. Each visit helped me to understand and deal with matters more competently, and the main point was learning to understand why he would say things and how we should respond. What was most ideal about it was everything said was specifically tailored to David, rather than a general talk about children.

The next six months were filled with court appearances and Child Welfare meetings, interspersed with weekly or twice weekly visits from James with advice on Social Services input and to relieve us of our cake and tea supplies. Supervised contact with Jane, her mother and David was agreed in court, as well as Parental Responsibility for Annie. During one court appearance Adam Davies and Jane's brief debated with Judge Renhold the considerations of David's emotions in handling supervised contact with Jane. I was sat at the back of the courtroom, unaware that I was shaking my head in disbelief.

"Mr Moore is shaking his head, may I ask your opinion Mr Moore?" the judge asked.

I was moved that the judge I had previously held in such contempt finally put value on my views.

"Sir," I said casually, "David is ten years old. I believe we are applying adult considerations to a child's perspective. He will be delighted to see his mother regardless of whether it is supervised."

I was stunned when the judge agreed with me. The contacts were not regularly timed and often they occurred every other week or sometimes every three weeks. David was accompanied by a Social Services professional, usually collected from school and returned home to us after the contact. David handled things in a matter-of-fact manner. Tuesday evenings however proved to be a regular problem with him becoming upset. This corresponded with his attending the after school sports club, and we were concerned that Jane was using a friendship with one of the supervisors and the coach as an indirect conduit. I spoke with the person responsible for child welfare at the club and explained in detail what had happened in David's life. She was understanding and aware of the friendship between Jane and one of the staff. I do not think it was a coincidence that a short time later that the lady responsible for child welfare was replaced. When David had first been taken into care the sports club coach had commented to me that the "bloody Social Services should stay out of people's lives." At the time I had chosen not to challenge him.

I found it interesting that the parents of the other children at David's school were quick to accept Annie and I by including us in afterschool events and social evenings. I dreaded to think what they had been told about us, but they were clearly aware that not everything they had been told was true. In fact the headmaster later complimented us on having the bravery to front these events.

In December 2010 we attended a Family Group Conference. Their purpose is simple enough: based on a Maori tradition, the family gets together with supporters

who declare their main objective to be the best interest
of the child, and everyone thrashes out the issues to
determine a way forward. The idea sounded perfect; I
cannot recall who suggested the idea, but Social Services
and David's legal guardian Tanya Long followed it
through. A lady from another area, Angela, travelled
to see everyone concerned, explained the process and
arranged a date and venue. We were told that David
would be present throughout, and the concerns from
Annie and I that everyone present had to be made aware
of all the facts pertaining to the situation were met with
reassurances that everything would be transparent.

Plans were made, a date and venue established, and
we declared with prior notice the names of our intended
supporters. Jane, her mother and a couple of her female
friends were going to attend along with the male friend
she had at the Looked After Child Review. Annie and
I had a friend of mine, my brother, his wife, and a friend
of Annie's supporting. David had requested his cousin
accompany him as a supporter; he was now ten years
old and they had not seen each other for many years,
with their relationship only re-established since David
came to live with us. David's headmaster had also kindly
offered to support him.

When we arrived I was surprised to see that Jane's
new partner Graham was there, despite not being on
the list of supporters. His mother was also there as
"supporter to Jane's mother".

Social Services had assigned yet another officer to
David's case because the second had also now gone on
maternity leave. The new one was also female and closer
in age to Annie and I. We were all sat around the meeting
room with refreshments laid on a table to one side.

Angela introduced herself and explained the aims of the conference. She then asked everyone to introduce themselves individually. Once that was out of the way, the Social Services officer explained why David had been taken into care; when she got to the point of explaining that his mother had emotionally abused him, David burst into tears. It broke my heart to see, and it annoyed me that he had been put in this situation after Annie and I had said multiple times that he should not be present for the first half of the meeting. I had been instructed not to explain to him the reason why he was taken into care, to let him figure things out by himself as he got older, and now it had been laid bare by strangers. I was even more annoyed when, witnessing David's distress, the Social Services officer ceased her explanation and left us to begin the conference. I was at a loss to how we could discuss David's future when not everyone knew all the information. Among the important things omitted from the explanation were the fictitious illnesses David had been subjected to, and which had been a major issue in the court process when determining he should be removed from his mother.

"Stop looking so angry," Annie whispered in my ear, but I couldn't. The meeting had been arranged with great expectations and assurances, but within the first few minutes the organisation had failed. I have always said, and will always maintain, that my son should enjoy a full relationship with his entire family. But I was at a loss to how I could uphold that in a debate with people who had not heard officially that Jane had been found guilty of manipulating David's health. My supporters knew of the situation, but they should still have heard it officially to know that I wasn't putting a spin on it.

At this and several other meetings any attempt by Annie or myself to explain a situation by making reference to the past was dismissed with the statement "The past is in the past we now need to move forward". But we would always ask, "How is it possible to move forward if the past is not recognised and responsibilities acknowledged?"

My brother started the discussions by making small talk and saying what a fine boy David was. Graham then chipped in by asking how we could get more time for Jane with David. One of Jane's supporters then said we might agree that David should be able to see both his parents equally whenever he wanted to. I had to bite my tongue, because I wanted to ask them if they had made such a suggestion to Jane a couple of years ago when I was fighting in court to see him.

For our part, Annie and I agreed to every common sense proposal, but with the simple provision that "certain criteria must be met", namely that Jane should actively and positively engage with the Social Services Child in Need plan and seek help for both her behaviour and to understand what David was going through. It wasn't long before David understandably became upset, and his headmaster took him and his cousin out of the room for a while.

The subject of communication between Jane and myself was discussed, and I explained that I was willing to communicate with her in writing only. Jane's supporters dismissed this as ridiculous, so I reminded them of the number of times Jane had made false accusations of assault.

"You assaulted her father," Graham accused me.

I was furious – this was another lie that could only have originated from Jane. "You are wrong Graham.

I have never assaulted anyone, but Jane's father has threatened me on numerous occasions."

My supporter then wisely suggested that he and I leave the room.

Angela, the social worker, and David's guardian Tanya Long were in a separate room talking. When I walked in they asked what had happened.

"Graham has accused me of assaulting Jane's father."

"Sorry to hear that but don't worry Mr Moore; it's all part of the debating process," Angela reasoned.

"Why was there no mention of David's health issues in the introduction?" I asked.

"My role is to protect David. I had no choice but to stop when he became distressed."

"Annie and I insisted David not be present at least for the first half of the first meeting," I countered, to no reply.

I calmed down and returned to the meeting.

"A child needs its mother," Graham's mother asserted.

"Have you read the paediatrician's report?" I asked.

She waved her hand dismissively, as though she had read it but it was irrelevant.

"Plenty of children were raised after the war with no father," Jane's mother said incredulously, and all the supporters jumped in to point out that had been a tragic and unavoidable situation.

The meeting had degenerated into a shambles with no focus, and Jane sat as supercilious as she had at the LAC Review. When it got round to discussing Christmas contact for David and Jane, three possible scenarios were given with the title of *David's Wish List*:

1. David spends Christmas Day with Annie and I, then he gets dropped off with his mother

between four and five o'clock in the afternoon. He stays overnight with his mother then he gets returned home between four and five o'clock the following afternoon.

2.	David gets dropped off with his mother between four and five o'clock on Christmas Day afternoon and is returned by nine o'clock the same evening.

3.	Same as option 2, but he goes back to his mother's the following morning until five o'clock in the afternoon.

It was finally agreed that Christmas Day contact would be four hours, and there would be supervised contact during the school holidays. This meant I would have my second Christmas with my son since he had been born, and the first one in nine years.

The wish list ended in shared parenting, fifty-fifty, with an informal arrangement that David would see Jane whenever he wanted. It was something that myself and Annie both hoped could be achieved, especially for David but it would also give us some more time to ourselves again.

The meeting lasted about three hours in total, and I think for David it was a positive, albeit emotional, experience. He was upbeat afterwards and although he had some questions for me, he was not upset and settled into bed easily.

The irony of it all was that his wish list was everything I had ever wanted, but given the history together with the level of delusion, denial and lies from Jane and her mother, I was unable to recommend progress to be anything more than slow and closely monitored, for fear that David would go back to being systematically abused.

CHAPTER 20

The final hearing took place in January 2011, although I thought that 'final herring' would be a better turn of phrase because it isn't final at all. The word gives you false hope that this will be the end, that after a decade of turmoil and struggling the battles will finally cease, but it doesn't mean that at all.

It was a school day and the hearing was to take place in the city, an hour and a half away from where we lived. We realised just how little family structure we had around us at that stage in our lives: both mine and Annie's parents had passed away, our children were living abroad or working, and we had no friends with children of David's age. My niece was the closest family member with a son the same age as David. On this occasion, however, we were stuck. I had called David's school the previous day to explain that we may be back late from court. The receptionist told me that he could stay in the library for an hour or so after his lessons ended.

With that arranged we dropped him off a few minutes early in the morning and drove to the city to meet Rebecca at her offices. We had planned to arrive an hour before the court hearing would start, to give us time to go through the details. However, city traffic and finding somewhere to park meant we were a few minutes late. As we ran to her office the large mug of tea I had before leaving home made its presence known; looking at my watch I decided to forgo the convenience of the multiple fast food restaurants that we passed, instead opting to just use the facilities at Rebecca's office.

When we got there we approached the reception desk and were politely directed to take a seat because Rebecca was "in conference."

"Can you tell me where the bathrooms are please?" I asked.

"We do not have any available for clients, sir."

There's nothing like being denied the possibility of using a bathroom to make a person feel like a young child again. I looked at Annie. "I think I will run back to one of the fast food restaurants and use the toilet there," I suggested.

"Tom, we are already late," she said in a tone that I had not heard since my mother was alive.

There was no use arguing – every man, be he a husband or son, knows that tone and the futility of arguing against it – so I took a seat and, trying not to squirm, quietly counted the minutes.

Fifteen.

Twenty.

Surely she's going to arrive soon?

Twenty-five minutes.

It was just shy of an hour when Rebecca finally appeared, with the advocates of the case congregating behind her.

"Sorry for the delay," she said. "There were discussions on the case that had to be addressed before the hearing."

"That's okay Rebecca, not a problem. Before we start, is there a toilet around here I can use?"

Rebecca addressed the receptionist and asked her to let me through to the staff bathroom.

A few minutes later I was relieved, but we now had to dash to the court building with Rebecca briefing us as we went. We would have to put a schedule of proposed contact for David and Jane, which would most probably be contested and then we would enter a debate to try to reach a compromise between Jane and ourselves. If we were unable to agree then the judge would make a decision, and we were told this was not the best option.

Karen had advised us to insist on supervised contact until David reached sixteen and to request a 91.14 order to prevent the matter returning to court. Rebecca thought this was not possible.

"What have the advocates been discussing earlier?" I asked.

"We had to agree on how Andrew Green's bill is to be allocated to each party," she explained.

"But as everything is funded by the taxpayer why does it matter whose name it goes under?"

"It has to be agreed who stands what percentage of the fee to their account."

I decided not to say anything and instead started a mental tally of approximate costs to the taxpayer that had been amassed just from the advocates deciding how to account for the expense of the Psychologist report. My conclusion was that Andrew's bill would have been able to pay for a high-spec, quality German car, and the advocates had spent another ten per cent agreeing which avenues should be used to channel the costs. Their discussions on dividing financial matters had taken priority over my bladder and the need for us to be fully briefed on what was about to happen in a final hearing ten years in the waiting.

We had been to city court several times since David had been taken into care, because Judge Renhold had been determined to keep tabs on the case and this was the most convenient venue for him to do so. We spotted Jane and Graham outside, and noted that while Graham now accompanied Jane to court he never actually entered the building. We surmised he was being kept at a distance, unlike Jane's previous friend who had been in the waiting room and discovered much more was going on than Jane had admitted. We cleared security in the court, which was comparable to taking a trans-Atlantic flight – unlike our hometown, where a lone security guard would wave a technological wand around your body and maybe rummage through your bag if you weren't personal acquaintances.

The waiting area was filled with people sorting out their individual problems, it was confusing and difficult to find who you needed to be talking to. Rebecca ushered us into a private room and explained there would be a lot of discussion happening prior to going in front of the judge. I interpreted this as meaning we would be bartering until we reached an agreement. Rebecca then disappeared to discuss matters with the legal represent-atives of Jane and David, returning a short while later with the news that Jane now had a barrister in addition to her usual brief – at the taxpayers' expense. Each court appearance required a minimum of two, and sometimes up to four, Social Services staff, plus their legal team; David had a legal guardian and solicitor, Annie and I had Rebecca, and Jane had a solicitor and a barrister. In addition, Social Services needed a full day to travel to and from court, plus preparations, and then there was the usher and the judge. With all that taken into account, I shudder to think what each appearance amounted to.

Rebecca and the advocates were adamant that we needed to come to a structured agreement for contact to happen and progress into a normal separated family situation, but Karen, Annie and I all doubted if there would ever come a time when David would not be used and have his divided loyalties manipulated by his mother. I had by this point accepted that she was incapable of change and David would just have to learn to understand her behaviour. My reasoning was that as long as she could not manipulate his health, we would battle through.

Rebecca finally returned to the private room and explained a compromise that she believed the judge would endorse. The suggestion was that David would see Jane unsupervised for a few hours once a week, then progress to overnight within a couple of months. It was not what we had hoped for but with a spirit of reconciliation, wanting to progress and fearing what the judge might order if we failed to agree, we accepted the proposal.

Shortly after, we filed into the courtroom and the agreement was read out to Judge Renhold. All was sounding fine, until Item 8, which stated that further contact could go ahead with the agreement of both parties. I was alarmed to hear this because it had not been agreed with Rebecca. I whispered to her, and she assured me this was standard in final contact orders. Standard or not, Annie and I were unhappy; we would not have agreed to the proposal had we known because we were both aware that this would be the key for Jane to manipulate things again. Unfortunately, there wasn't anything we could do about it now.

With everything concluded, we left the court and rushed back home to collect David from school on time, without him having to stay late.

We had been home for two hours when the phone rang. It was Jane, asking to amend the schedule of contact we had only just agreed to. I diplomatically told her that it was impossible. I had a feeling this was the start of things to come.

When the first unsupervised contact came around, it was for a few hours at Jane's house, with the condition that she would collect David and return him home. About half an hour before he was due back, the phone rang. It was David, asking to stay longer because he got into a game of Monopoly. Jane was well aware that she was not to allow such a situation, but she had again put me in an awkward position. She had created a problem to invoke a reaction, allowing her to relay the story to her supporters for sympathy and attention. I was on the spot: my choices were to agree, or be the bad guy. I told David he could stay another thirty minutes, but no longer. Jane had done it again.

When David arrived home he quoted Item 8, and declared that he would be seeing Jane "lots more". My concerns over Item 8 in court had been justified, and now I was worried just how much of a mess would be created. James, the Family Support Worker, was still assigned to us, so I asked him to explain to David that this would not be the case. James was happy to oblige; he told David that things had to remain as the order had stated, and he told me later that David had been quite resistant to the idea. I was thankful it wasn't me that had to tell him.

Sadly, but not unsurprisingly, there then began a series of tearful nights with David trying to understand what was happening and why. I assured him that his entire family loved him and none of this was his fault.

These were distressing times for us all.

Annie usually left me to talk to David alone, but she was concerned that I may start to go too far in explaining things, so when he was distressed she stayed close by. I called Karen multiple times and we discussed in detail what could (and should not) be said to David, and our visits with CAMHS were also helpful. I chose not to mention about working with Karen, but their advice was similar to Karen's anyway.

On the second contact the same thing happened again, but this time I refused an extension and told David he had to be home by the agreed time. He was not happy, but returned promptly. I then reasoned with him and pacified him easily enough by explaining that the order was from the court, and had to be followed. I then wrote a letter to Jane telling her how disappointed I was that she had David phone me when she knew she should not be doing so, and that she needed to stop using him as a conduit. There was no reply to the letter, and instead she started to use David indirectly.

Shortly after, progress in the contact meant that Jane was supposed to have David for tea and then drop him off at the after school sports club. The condition was that she would leave him after dropping him off, but instead of doing so, she stayed to watch him play. What was troubling was not so much that she decided to watch him play, but that rather than sit in the spectators' area, she pulled a chair into the hall and sat right beside David as he played his game. No one from the centre confronted her over it.

I was scheduled to collect David at a set time, and when I arrived I saw Jane parked in a chair right beside him, effectively hindering him. I stayed away from them as I had noticed David acknowledge my arrival, so I waited patiently until it was time to go. Ten minutes later, David was still talking to Jane, so I was forced to inform him that we had to leave.

As we drove away from the centre we passed Jane, walking home in the rain. I was frustrated because both David and I had been manipulated once again, and I would again be the bad guy for collecting him away from his mother and then not offering her a lift home.

The following week David's team was scheduled to play a match against another club from across town, who cancelled at the last minute. Jane was informed of this on arrival to the centre, and she then sent me a text saying David would need to be collected early. I ignored the text because I knew that it was standard procedure for the club to continue as usual, and the children would simply play games amongst themselves.

When I turned up to collect David, I found him sat with Jane ready to go, while many of the other kids were still playing.

"Why did you ignore Mum's text?" David asked firmly when he got into the car.

"There was just no reason to reply," I said. I started to get angry with Jane's insistence of continually stirring trouble. A friend of mine once said that Jane would make trouble in an empty house.

It was becoming difficult for me to stick to my belief that we would be fine so long as Jane was unable to manipulate David's health, and her actions were also frustrating Annie. I knew this was the desired effect that Jane wanted, so I sent her another letter, where I explained that she was using David as an indirect conduit and she must adhere to the instructions of the contact order.

During this same period a friend and supporter of mine had been attempting a communication link, as suggested at the Family Group Conference, via one of Jane's supporters. However, each time it was attempted something was twisted or misinterpreted and Jane's supporter blamed me. I found out that when my supporter tried to reason with Jane's supporter that Jane had abused David, it was argued that Jane's entire legal team, including the barrister, had been useless. The party line was essentially that Jane was innocent and a better team would have proven that. My supporter stated that it was futile to continue further attempts at such communication; I agreed, but was grateful for him at least trying.

It didn't seem long before it was time for David to stay over with his mother. It appeared to go well when he returned home, until he went to bed. He had regressed to needing the bedroom door left open at a precise angle, the light left on, lavender sprayed on each of his pillows and reassuring visits from me every few minutes to ensure he was still okay. This was heartbreaking, because all of our efforts had been undone in one night. I discussed the matter with Social Services, who then made several attempts to set up a meeting with Jane to address the issues. It was like being back in time, because whenever Social Services suggested it, Jane insisted she was unavailable. She did agree on one occasion, and arrived with a legal representative. Social Services stated that if Jane attended the meeting with a representative, they would also need one and so would I. Neither Annie nor myself was interested in having legal representation though, so Social Services tried to persuade Jane to attend without it herself. She refused, so the meeting ended up being cancelled. Thankfully, within a week we had managed to restore David's normal bedtime routine.

We also noticed how David had recently become obsessed with counting calories, and working out how many he would burn off with various activities. My first thought was that he was simply learning about dietary values at school.

"Did you notice that when we were on holiday he had not wanted to uncover himself? He seemed very conscious of his weight," Annie had said to me. He in no way needed to lose weight; he had been incredibly skinny when he came to live with us and had put on some much needed weight. Later we discovered that Jane was attempting to lose weight, and we couldn't see that it was simply a coincidence.

When it was time for David's second overnight stay with his mother, he returned with his own lavender bag. At bedtime he proudly showed me the bag and said: "Mum gave me this, to help me sleep." Once again, we needed the light on, the door at a specific angle and repeated reassuring.

"You know, David, you don't need the lavender bag to sleep properly," I told him, but I didn't try to stop him from putting it under his pillow anyway.

I contacted Karen the next day and explained to her what had happened. She was alarmed: "I am very concerned then that Jane is very close to regaining control over David's belief of health issues," she said.

This, in turn, put me on alert, so I contacted Social Services again, who immediately called round to the house to discuss the matter fully. They shared Karen's point of view, as did CAMHS when we visited for an appointment a few days later.

I decided to seek the opinions of all the professionals that had been involved, to ask them if I should cease contact with David and his mother. Karen's opinion was that I should do what I deemed necessary to protect David: "It's true to say that there's no proof Jane poisoned David, it is strongly suspected that she did. But there is also no doubt that she poisoned him mentally against his paternal family, which damaged him emotionally."

CAMHS later put it to me in a simple phrase: "As we see it, it's not a case of if you stop contact, but when."

I took this to mean they understood I was running out of patience on how much I was going to let Jane continue to affect David. I phoned Andrew Green and asked his opinion. "It's highly unlikely that Jane will ever acknowledge what she has done to David and change her behaviour," he told me.

Annie and I also discussed the matter in great detail; we knew that if we stopped contact, we would be accused of sour grapes by anyone who did not fully understand the situation – which was the majority of people. Annie was as loyal as ever and told me she would support me whatever I decided. Having spoken to everyone I could, I knew that I had no choice but to halt contact between David and Jane. I knew this because I had battled against her for a decade and I was aware that no matter how much I bent to make allowances or keep things peaceful, she would not be content with a middle ground. My philosophy had to be one of zero tolerance when it came to David's health, and Jane's role in his health.

I called Rebecca to get advice on the legal angles; I explained the events including the lavender bag and with no hesitation she told me to stop contact. "That woman is downright wicked, she needs to learn a lesson," were her exact words.

That same afternoon I composed a letter to Jane advising her of the opinions and concerns of the professionals regarding such things as the lavender bag. I informed her that I was stopping contact between her and her son until she demonstrated she had sought to address her issues and a radical change of behaviour. My decision was not to teach Jane a lesson – I knew that was impossible – but to do the best by my son, which meant maintaining a safe upbringing in a stable environment.

Writing the letter was easy, but my next task was telling David of my decision and that was far from simple. When I told him the news he was angry and disappointed; I had anticipated both emotions but it hurt me deeply to see him so confused and upset. I tried to explain the reason to him calmly but I was not pacifying him at all, and it was made much harder from the fact that there was a lot of information I was simply not allowed to tell him. That put me in the awkward situation of not being able to tell him the reason why I had to make such a decision, and try to find something else to tell him.

I also realised in that moment that in his entire life, no one had lost their temper with David. He had always been consoled calmly and plans had been adjusted to suit him. He always had his own way and was allowed to win any games he played, so he was now in serious need of being taken out of his comfort zone as often as possible to prevent him developing him into an unpleasant, arrogant adult.

Realising this, I changed tactic with David. I raised my voice and matched his angry tone. "Do you not think I'm disappointed? I've jumped through every hoop, I have done exactly as I have been told, repeatedly, and your mother has not done a single damned thing to make your life easier and give *you* any consideration."

David did not break down or get angrier. He looked at me, but I knew I was having an impact.

"Do you think you were taken away from your mother for no good reason?" I continued. "Your mother was given countless chances over many months to put you first and halt any risk of you being taken away from her, but she did nothing." I stopped to let David absorb what he had just been told. I knew that I was crossing the lines that Karen had told me I should stay firmly within, and had Annie overheard she would have called me out of the room to tell me to stop immediately.

David wept a little, but his demeanour looked to have improved. What I said clearly stuck in his mind, because when he went to bed that night he said, "My mother has never done anything wrong."

"Why were you ill so often when you lived with her, David?" I asked in a matter-of-fact tone.

"I was really ill; really ill Dad."

"Yes, son, you were really ill. Now can you tell me why you have not been ill once since you went to live with Dana and Jeff?" I let him ponder the question for a while, then changed my tone: "I love you son. Your mum has a problem that I cannot begin to explain to you. Since you came to live with us you've known I've always wanted you to love your mum."

David nodded in agreement.

"But your mum didn't want you to know and love me. Love for family cannot be measured, it is not up to me or anyone else to say who you should or should not love. You love your mum, yes?"

"Yes," he agreed.

"And you love your grandma, yes?"

David nodded.

"But you don't love your mum any less because you love your grandma, do you?"

"No," he said, understanding what I was getting at.

"Your mum's idea is that you only have a bucketful of love to give, and if you give some to someone else then there is less for her, but that's not right, is it David?"

"No," he agreed.

The conversation had turned out remarkably well and I was pleased that he had been so mature in listening to what I said. I knew that there was a lot going on in his head, so I reassured him that I would do everything possible to restore contact between him and his mother as soon as possible. In my heart, though, I knew that would not be easy.

Some weeks later we received a letter from a newly appointed firm of solicitors that were working for Jane, stating that they had been hired because of difficulty she was having in maintaining contact with her son, and that "most of those difficulties" were emanating from me. The letter asked for a list of problems I believed existed and what my proposed resolution would be.

I replied to the letter with a brief explanation of the history of the case, mentioning that David was taken into temporary foster care and that Jane had not opposed him living with me. I explained that David had been seeing Jane regularly and they were able to talk on the phone whenever they wanted, but that Jane had broken the conditions of the court order and alarmed the professionals because of her influence on David. I finished the letter by stating that Jane needs to consult with both myself and Annie before giving ideas to David, as well as seeking the help of other professionals to address the problems that David was experiencing.

Coincidentally, and unknown to the branch, one of the firm's associates was the solicitor Bob Cronin had engaged to act for David some years earlier. She was the woman who had sent a number of letters but failed to do anything constructive. Our reply to the firm received no response, but we figured that Jane had been obliged to seek new representation on the basis of her supporters' opinions that her usual brief was incompetent.

A short time later we received a court order application for contact from her original firm of solicitors. Evidently the new solicitors had not told Jane what she wanted to hear.

Social Services arranged for Jane and a supporter to meet with Annie, myself, and my brother, who was acting as my supporter, to discuss making progress with restoring contact. The Social Services officer who had managed the Family Group Conference was present and took notes throughout. Jane's supporter was the friend who had insulted the headmaster throughout the Looked After Child (LAC) Review.

The meeting started with the officer suggesting we deal with the problems that arose from the attempted return to contact.

"On the very first unsupervised contact, why did you allow David to call me to ask if he could stay longer?" I asked Jane.

The response was a waffled rambling that avoided giving an answer.

I repeated the question: "Why did you allow David to call me to ask if he could stay longer?"

Again Jane avoided the question. Her supporter finally interrupted and accused me of being belligerent and not being objective.

I raised my voice and repeated the question again. I wanted an answer.

Jane's supporter incredulously raised an objection to the Social Services officer that I was being aggressive.

My brother countered: "Tom has been through ten years of hell. Jane disobeyed the instructions given to her, he deserves an answer." He was dismissed.

I raised my voice again: "I want an answer to the question, otherwise I will take it that no effective communication will take place today and the meeting will be over."

There was a silence before Jane stammered: "He was adamant he wanted to call you."

"You knew you were not allowed to let that happen," I said.

Jane repeated her last statement.

"So you are not capable of asserting parental authority?" I challenged.

Her supporter leapt to her rescue and called me ridiculous. He said a lot that contradicted the reports from the psychologist and paediatrician, so Annie stepped in: "Your supporter appears to be misinformed Jane, doesn't he?"

Jane denied comment.

Annie repeated her statement, with the addition: "I think you should correct him."

Jane stayed silent again. Her supporter continued his ignorant tirade, ridiculing the psychologist and paediatrician reports until my brother told him to be quiet so Jane could answer. He ignored the request. My brother was getting frustrated, and when Jane's supporter began to ridicule the issue of the lavender bag I decided to step in firmly.

"Okay, let's say you are correct." He stopped talking and looked at me. "Let's say you're right, that the lavender bag was not cause for concern." I had his attention, but I could easily predict his answer to my next statement. "Whether you value them or not, given the conclusions of the reports, do you accept the concerns the lavender bag issue invokes on all the professionals charged with a duty of care for David?"

He dismissed this, and I even heard him say "coincidence."

I could not resist. "Coincidence? Like the Christmas Eve you coincidentally happened to appear when Jane was screaming 'I need help here'?"

This hit a nerve. He immediately denied anything had been planned that day. "It was a pure coincidence," he insisted.

Annie spoke out "Judge Renhold has repeatedly mentioned the frequency of coincidences in Jane's accounts. I think you both ought to acknowledge the concerns of the lavender bag, given the reports from the psychologist and paediatrician."

"The reason David was taken into care was because you lied to the psychologist," Jane asserted.

"Can you repeat that Jane?" I asked, "I want to make sure we heard you correctly so the officer can note it down."

"I said, the reason David was taken into care was because you lied to the psychologist," she repeated, with her supporter agreeing.

I considered the meeting to be over now; there was just no point in being there.

Before I could say anything though, my brother stood up. He apologised to Annie and I saying he had to leave the room and as he walked past Jane's supporter he said, "You are a very small, sad man."

I looked at Annie and told her I considered the meeting to be a waste of time. I looked at the Social Services officer, who had overheard me, and said: "I was hoping to hear some acknowledgement of responsibility, maybe a few promises to stick to the rules, but that isn't ever going to happen is it?" I stood up to leave and when I reached the door I saw Annie was still sitting down and arguing with Jane and her supporter. I walked out, granting Annie her wish to express her feelings towards Jane.

As I closed the door behind me I heard Jane plead to Annie to convince me to let her see her son, "As one mother to another."

I knew those words would strike a chord with Annie – she would give no quarter, having been sat in the Family Group Conference while Jane and her mother put outrageous spin on the breakup of her previous marriage.

I found my brother outside, waiting for me. "Sorry I had to leave, but I either knocked his head through the bloody wall or left the room, and I believe the latter is best for you," he said, shaking his head in disbelief.

"What were you doing ever letting that woman into your life?"

I shook my head too, but said nothing. He was right, I had been a fool for allowing Jane into my life. I deserved a bollocking, but David did not deserve any of it.

Annie joined us moments later, reeling from the encounter. "As one mother to another! Can you believe it? After all she has accused me of and the rumours she's spread about me."

Karen, Andrew Green and CAMHS had, together with all the Social Services staff involved, told us that it was highly unlikely Jane was capable of changing. I owed it to David to at least try every avenue, but to no avail.

A short while later Annie and I were once again in court, in front of Judge Renhold. Jane's brief had made an application to uphold the existing contact order, just as I had years earlier. Judge Renhold began proceedings by stating how disappointed he was that we were in front of him again. He passed glances around each person present and I maintained eye contact with him as he looked at me.

Jane's brief set a low tone, by saying that we had unjustly stopped contact because of unsubstantiated claims. When he had finished his speech, the judge addressed me to explain our actions.

I clarified what had happened: the phone call from Jane to change the order hours after the final hearing, the phone call from David asking to extend the contact hours on the very first meeting, the letters I had written to Jane telling her to stop using David as a conduit.

"May I see a copy of the letters?" Judge Renhold requested.

I handed them to him.

Renhold read them all then addressed Jane: "Can I read your replies?"

"I didn't reply to them," she stated.

"Why did you not respond?" Judge Renhold asked.

"I refuse to respond to such a tone of letter."

"I see nothing wrong with the tone," Judge Renhold said.

I had been careful in writing the letters, having taken advice from Karen and James. It was important to avoid pleasantries or small talk and just stick to the facts.

"I see these as clear and concise," the judge continued. "What in these letters do you not understand?"

Jane did not reply.

"You were not supposed to allow David to get involved with arrangements, yet you did and Mr Moore in this letter points out your failure of this requirement and informs you to stop immediately. I see nothing wrong in these letters."

Jane's brief tried to navigate away from the topic by rambling about the lavender bag and dismissing it as inconsequential. Judge Renhold looked at me for response.

I explained how David had been manipulated at the sports club evenings and I had been made out as the bad guy each time.

Judge Renhold nodded his head. "So you are continually put in a situation where you are obliged to agree to her requests or David sees you as being in the wrong?"

"Yes, sir," I replied, then explained how David had returned home with the lavender bag saying: "Mum gave me this to help me sleep" and how I had then sought the help of all the professionals involved. "I did not take the decision lightly, but based on the advice of the professionals and with sincere regret that such action has been necessary." I anticipated the judge requesting to see written evidence of the professionals' opinions, so I openly admitted to not having anything in writing before concluding: "Sir, I consider my son to be just as much at risk of harm from his mother today as he was the day after he was taken into care."

The judge looked at Jane's brief and raised both eyebrows. I had played the card Jane had used repeatedly to keep me out of David's life, except I had proof of my claim.

Judge Renhold reflected for a moment and then addressed Jane: "Do you understand the concerns of the professionals?"

"There is no need for concern. The lavender bag was a free gift from a supermarket promotion on a brand of washing liquid." She should have stopped there, but to the amazement of the court she continued: "David knows very well that I keep lavender bags in the draw with my underwear, it keeps my knickers smelling fresh."

The courtroom was shocked – even her brief was stunned. Judge Renhold's jaw almost hit the table and he struggled to find words. "Well," he said with a vacant stare at the microphone in front of him, "these proceedings are being recorded and, given the last statement, I see no alternative than to uphold Mr and Mrs Moore's actions. I will be reinstating David's legal guardian and representation."

CHAPTER 21

With Adam Davies and Tanya Long now reinstated, Tanya visited us on several occasions to determine exactly what the situation was. Her job was made more difficult because Jane had deliberately confused her by saying that David did not need his bedroom door at a certain angle, the lights left on or his pillows sprayed with lavender in order to sleep. The denial didn't work very well though, because when Tanya asked David himself he confirmed it to be true.

Both Tanya and Adam shared the concerns of the other professionals regarding the lavender bag, and they arranged a meeting with Jane, Tanya, Annie and I to discuss matters, including that of moving things forward.

This period of time happened to be the run-up to David's birthday, and we were starting to make party plans. Annie organised the invites and we booked the local Laser Quest venue as we had the year before.

At that previous party, one of David's friends, the son of a friend of Jane, had attended. He had been dropped off outside and his mother waited in the car during the party, refusing to enter the building. We sent an invite to the same friend for the upcoming party, and I received a text message from the mother a couple of days later:

Sorry. Charlie can't make it this year. We hope to see David very soon with his mum. Tom, do you

185

ever stop to think of the consequences your actions may bring? Do you not ever consider what untold emotional damage you are doing to David in preventing him from seeing his mum? Jane has never done anything to hurt that poor boy. And never prevented him from seeing you. It was David who was terrified of you thanks to your bullying behaviour when he was little. You know that. So why don't you give up this wicked, selfish behaviour and let the poor kid see his mum again? You are now far more guilty of emotional abuse than Jane ever was.

My initial reaction was to be angry but soon realised that her remarks were testament to Jane's continued denial. This woman's outlook also confirmed a profile similar to Jane's in that she was willing to deny her son a friendship with David. I wanted to write to her and ask for justification on disagreeing with all the professionals involved in the case. I also wanted to know how she could deny her son a friendship and accuse me of bullying behaviour when she had never seen me with David, other than when he was a few months of age. There was a lot I wanted to ask, and even more I wanted to explain, but I refrained.

Instead I issued myself a cooling off period, after which I decided to do nothing other than show the text message to Tanya. She was shocked at what was said, and explained to me that this did a lot of damage to Jane's case.

With the party plans sorted, we then had to arrange how David could see his mother and grandmother on his birthday. Social Services were no longer involved to the degree of offering supervision of contact, so it was something we needed to work out by ourselves.

One evening I dropped David off at the sports club and I was asked into the office by Barbara, a club assistant and a teacher at the school, who I knew Jane had befriended and convinced that David living with me was the result of a miscarriage of justice. I did not want to be alone with this woman so I asked another female assistant to join us.

"Jane has asked me to supervise contact on David's birthday," Barbara said.

Before I could respond the other assistant immediately spoke up addressing both Barbara and myself: "We don't get involved with any personal issues. We have to remain entirely neutral and the child's best interests are to be paramount."

"Yes," said Jane's friend. "This is not me taking sides, Mr Moore. I would just be helping a friend, and putting David's best interest first."

I thought for a second on how to respond diplomatically but firmly. "I'm sorry, but please don't get involved. There is a lot more to the situation than you, or a lot of people, realise. As a teacher at David's school, please also bear in mind that the same local authority that employs you had David taken into care." That was the best I could do to remain calm while making it clear that she would be compromising herself.

Nonetheless, my response evidently had no impact because she continued by saying that she wanted to "help" David. The other assistant was visibly concerned at the lack of neutrality in her colleague, but she made no difference either. In the end, I left the office stating clearly and simply, "Please do not get involved."

Tanya arranged a meeting on a late afternoon in the local CAFCASS offices. Annie and I arrived and were greeted by the same officer I had years earlier accused of being incompetent; aside from the initial eye contact as he answered the door, he didn't look me in the eye again. As we passed through the building to a meeting room, I wondered if he had learned anything from the mistakes he and the system had made.

A few minutes later Tanya walked in, and Jane arrived shortly after. The discussion began with Tanya asking why David had been allowed to call me requesting to extend contact when Jane knew it was prohibited. As was typical in these discussions, Jane waffled and skirted around an answer. Frustrated by the lack of an explanation, Tanya pushed further, asking how David came home quoting Item 8 of the court order verbatim. Jane shrugged her shoulders and denied any influence in the matter, silently suggesting that David found and memorised it by himself. Tanya then asked why Jane had gone to the after school sports club and sat beside David as he played, when she knew she was only meant to drop him off. Once more Jane uttered a meaningless response. Tanya then addressed the text message from Jane's friend, reading it out in its entirety. Jane shrugged her shoulders once more, uttering: "I'm not responsible for the actions of my friends."

"But surely this action can only have come about because of what you have told your friend," Tanya insisted.

Jane denied she had any influence and stated she had neither seen nor spoken to that friend in over a year.

"Jane," Annie spoke up, "this friend was at the Family Group Conference six months ago."

Jane shrugged. "Six months or twelve is of no consequence."

Tanya took this moment to read an excerpt from Andrew Green's report: "Jane must accept responsibility for the opinions of her friends".

"It wasn't my doing and it isn't my concern," Jane replied.

It was apparent to everyone, except Jane, that she was confirming she had not and would not change. This meeting ended with David's legal guardian defending our actions in stopping contact and declaring to be on board with Karen's advice to keep him free from Jane's influence for as long as possible.

David's birthday party was a success. A number of his friends turned up, and later in the day we took David to a local family pub to see his mother and grandmother. I used to take David to the same pub when he was smaller, to have fun on the play area while we had tea with my father, so it was a place he knew well. Social Services endorsed the plan, as did Tanya, who had no other suggestions on how to make contact successful.

My brother and his wife joined Annie and I in taking David to the pub. Jane was already sitting at a table with her mother and Barbara, the assistant from the after school sports club who wanted to supervise the contact. I remained silent, and the contact went well. Tanya later queried Jane as to the presence of the sports club assistant, and Jane replied that she "just happened" to be there.

Karen, along with several other professionals, had advised me many times that Jane was a clever woman who knew exactly what to do to get a reaction out of me. Social Services workers had told me repeatedly that I "need to learn how to handle her", and they were correct.

It soon became obvious that the legal process had no chance of protecting David from Jane, and he would have to learn how to understand and handle her. Tanya and Adam explained that the process would be required to move forward, which I found ironic considering it had never worked that way for me when I had been trying to see my son. "Judge Renhold wants to see steps forward and will expect to be given a schedule of how we see things progressing towards restoring contact," Tanya informed me.

"How much did Andrew Green's report cost?" I asked her.

Tanya raised her eyebrows and nodded her head to demonstrate acknowledgement that it was a large sum of money.

"And he described what Jane has subjected David to as far worse than physical abuse?"

Tanya nodded again.

"So now the report has been used to remove David from his abuser, the findings are no longer relevant?"

I methodically went through what I regard as a further obscene failure of Family Law, in that if Jane had physically abused David she would have been arrested. Yet, she had done what a professional had deemed "far worse" with no recourse from the system other than her child being taken away from her care. I was sure that Jane was using this fact to defend herself to friends. In the absence of proof of harm from me, Family Law, together with Jane's perjury, saw me effectively removed from David's life despite all the evidence that he was actually being abused at home. Now, with reports and stacks of evidence of Jane's instability and the suffering she caused David, plus failed contact time and repeated demonstrations that Jane had no desire to change her behaviour, Family Law was expecting us to move forward and restore contact.

It was not possible for Jane to be ordered, by law, to accept help. It was deemed pointless to order it because it was unlikely to have any effect unless the abuser recognises they need to change and actively engages with the process. While all the professionals recognised Jane's need for help, they were also urging us to "move forward" to restore contact.

Tanya was nodding throughout my dialogue, and then I asked: "So if Jane had originally hit David and following the final hearing hit him again, would Judge Renhold be expecting us to move forward with contact?" I knew what the answer was.

Tanya confirmed the failures of the system we were trapped within, and agreed that Jane had done far worse than hitting David. She even said that, "if Jane had broken David's arm it would be easier to defend in court." The conclusion was that the legal process could not protect David from "far worse than physical abuse" and so the only hope was that he would grow to understand and develop resilience to overcome his mother's personality disorder.

It was a logic that neither Annie nor I could understand. After all, if a child is physically abused we do not expect it to attend a self-defence class so that contact can be reinstated with the abuser, but that was the equivalent of what we were being told for our situation. There was nothing that I could say or do though; we had to make a move. The only thing I could think to do to benefit David was to play for as much time as possible. I shared this with Tanya who, with a tone and manner of someone exhausted of other ideas, concurred.

Annie and I agreed that David should see Jane, but only within a safe environment. Karen advised that we insist on supervised contact only and not crack under pressure. Social Services were no longer charged with responsibility to arrange supervision of contact and Tanya had no suggestions on how to provide supervision beyond personally doing so on an infrequent basis. James was no longer assigned to David's case – although he kept in touch and called by for updates periodically – but he had no suggestions other than to inform us that David was the worst case of abuse he had encountered so far, and that we should continue to ask what had changed since David was taken into care to justify a return to unsupervised contact. We did ask this question, and the only answer on each occasion was that David had grown up and changed, giving him a better chance of understanding what was going on. While this was indeed true, he was very fragile; it had been shown from the previous contacts that Jane had the key to undo all of our hard work and progress in mere minutes, and she had repeatedly shown no desire to change. We also could not subject friends or family to the potential consequences of trying to handle Jane, so we explored the possibilities of hiring qualified people that Karen knew, but being located over an hour away, the costs of supervision exceeded an amount that we could afford from our own pocket. We were unable to fund this, but we were rapidly reaching the deadline of appearing in court with a proposal for contact.

I suddenly thought of Dana and Jeff. They were perfectly suited for the job, they already knew David – in fact they had developed a wonderful rapport – and they had stayed in contact with us since David came to live with us. Better yet, they had David's trust and were fully briefed on the subject. I called and asked if they would help; they agreed without hesitation. All the professionals welcomed Dana and Jeff to supervising contact, although Jane, having spread vicious rumours about them, had no choice but to disapprove.

The next trip to court was considered a move in the right direction, with a schedule of supervised contact for the coming weeks. Judge Renhold was pleased with the proposition, and requested that Dana and Jeff be thanked for their commitment to David.

CHAPTER 22

I had made a point of ensuring that David spoke with his mother on the phone every two or three days, and Tanya supervised some contact sessions. It was difficult to monitor the content of the phone calls because I was trying to find the balance between giving David freedom and displaying trust in him, while not trusting Jane at all. I found it frustrating to see David face a barrage of questions, each time responding with "Yes Mum" and "No Mum", but we realised that it was easier to overcome the destabilising effect of the phone calls much easier than we could the unsupervised contact.

Since David had come to live with us I had re-established his relationship with his maternal aunt and her daughter Amanda. Several years earlier there had been a dispute on their side of the family and they had been cut off from Jane and her parents. One effect of this was these family members being spoken about negatively, so David had a very low opinion of them. When a relationship was rekindled, they were delighted to see David again and he reciprocated affection when he saw Annie and I treating them with a positive attitude. Amanda was particularly pleased; she had always loved David and now she made a point of making a fuss of him and spoiling him. She began to take him to the cinema and dinner once a week. When they returned one night

David hugged me and then Annie, as he walked upstairs to bed he said of Amanda, "She's lovely, isn't she Dad?" It was a surprising thing to hear him say, but what was most noticeable was the tone in which he had said it – like a realisation that was the opposite of what he had been told.

"Yes son, she is, and she loves you very much, as we all do," I replied.

I had been taking David to see Jane's mother on random occasions every week or fortnight for between ten and forty-five minutes at a time. I would drop him at her house and once I saw him enter I would drive to the supermarket or read for a while. I knew that this would receive a mixed reception, and Tanya was surprised by it.

"Why have you chosen to do this?" she asked me.

"David only has one remaining grandparent; he deserves to have a relationship with her at least." Tanya knew that I didn't like the woman, but David shouldn't suffer because of that, and I only ever said positive things about her to David. "I'm not doing it for her, I'm doing it for David."

"It is commendable of you, but how will you explain this to the judge when Jane's solicitor insists he should be seeing his mother under similar circumstances?" Tanya asked.

"The visits are unplanned and irregular so she can't arrange for Jane to be there, and if David returns with his head full of nonsense I can take time out to rectify that. Any normal person would realise a responsibility to ensure he has a positive experience or I won't be inspired to take him there again, and although I don't give her credit for having such common sense, I see it as worth the try for David's sake."

Tanya seemed happy with the explanation.

Much of the reason for voluntarily letting David see his grandmother was a lesson from my mother. In this situation she would have told me something like: "You are better than them. They can teach you nothing but how *not* to behave." That was a lesson that has always stuck with me, and I passed it on to my daughter one day as we were entering a shop. The person ahead of us had let the door swing back at us as we walked behind them, and Emily expressed her disgust at the lack of consideration.

"Have they taught you anything?" I asked her.

She looked at me with a face of confusion, and then smiled. "Yes, Dad, I never want to be rude or inconsiderate like they are." She never forgot the lesson either, and still to this day she holds doors open so much one may think she was employed to do so.

I was happy for David to see his grandmother so long as he was not at risk of harm. Jane had proven herself incapable of unsupervised contact and although her mother was in agreement with her on many issues, I did not think she could inflict the same emotional confusion on David as Jane could, and she had no chance of manipulating his health.

A few months later, in October of 2011, Annie, David and I took off for a month on an around the world trip to see Emily and Paul. David's school was understanding and gave permission for us to take David away for three weeks, coinciding with the one-week half-term holiday. The reason we had to go for so long is because everyone on my side of the family was eager for David to spend more time with his sister, and New Zealand is a bit far to go for a weekend visit.

While we were there we arranged for David to use the phone or Internet every few days to call his mother and grandmother. We met with my brother and sister-in-law in Australia, and broke the journey by spending a few days sailing in the Whitsunday Islands, where Emily's half-sister lives. David told me he wanted to try fishing, so we made a father-son bonding session of it and as luck would have it we even managed to catch a large tuna.

Several months before we were due to leave, David told Jane and her mother that he was going to be visiting Australia. A short while before we left there were a couple of emotional outbursts at bedtime, with him suddenly afraid of visiting Australia and me having to reassure him repeatedly that he would be safe at all times. I suspected the sudden fear was the result of Jane; she once told me, while she was under the influence of alcohol, an outrageously unbelievable story of how she had lost seven relatives in separate freak accidents in Australia – ranging from decapitation to drowning.

I contacted Tanya and told her of my frustration and suspicions that David was being deliberately scared to disrupt our travel plans. Tanya immediately contacted and questioned Jane and her mother, both of whom denied scaring David. Tanya then spoke with David and told him not to be afraid because he would be safe while there. Eventually David began insisting that we wouldn't actually be going to Australia, because we would mainly be on the islands off the coast. "We won't be in Australia, Dad, we'll be on the islands," he would say, and it seemed to console him.

While we were on holiday we had decided to move to a house with a garden and get a pet dog. When I was growing up we always had dogs, and I have particularly fond memories of one canine best friend we had from when I was ten until I was seventeen. Dogs were not a part of my life after that because I had always been travelling with work and lived in an apartment, but it seemed an appropriate time now. Annie was keen to have a garden and David was predictably overjoyed at the prospect of a pet, so we began the search for a new home.

After numerous disappointing viewings we saw a village house that Annie had found. We looked at the extensive garden and the multiple outbuildings, and Annie looked at me with a smile before we had even seen the main house in its entirety. I smiled back – we both loved the place. David loved it too, and, out of nowhere he suddenly decided to learn all he could about beekeeping.

The first contact with Dana and Jeff supervising was scheduled for early December, and a couple of hours before it was meant to begin I received a text message from Jane, telling me that Barbara, the sports club assistant and teacher I had told not to get involved, would be accompanying her.

"Contact is meant only for you, not anyone else," I responded. Despite my saying so, I had doubts that Jane would take notice of me, so I called the assistant directly to tell her to not get involved.

Barbara responded that she was simply "helping a friend" and acting in David's best interest,

"There is a lot more to the situation than you are aware of Barbara. David was only taken into care after extensive work from Social Services and an in-depth psychologist report. Anyone supervising him needs to be fully briefed on the situation to understand what his best interests are," I explained.

"I don't need a psychologist to understand what is going on," she insisted.

"Please Barbara, don't get involved. You can ask your colleagues at work for a full brief, or the previous headmaster at David's school," I reasoned.

Barbara then spewed a tirade of disrespect about the headmaster, so I reminded her that she was putting herself in a compromising situation – meaning, of course, her position at the sports club. She misinterpreted it and began screaming that I was threatening her job.

"I'm not doing any such thing, the only person threatening you is yourself. I just want you to realise that there is more to things than you know and you shouldn't be getting involved," I defended.

She then started a barrage of insults, accusing me of not acting in David's best interests and accusing me of threatening her. Eventually I apologised for phoning her and hung up, then sent Jane a text message affirming that no one other than herself was to be at the contact.

Over the Christmas period I sought the advice of the professionals, and all of them suggested I formally complain about Barbara and take David out of the sports club. I took issue with that though, because David loved the club and it would be unfair to him to take him away. I also figured that complaining would give Jane immense satisfaction, knowing that she had annoyed me, so I left it. Instead, I called the school and asked them to speak with Barbara.

This was just another demonstration of how Jane has an incredible ability to manipulate people, to the degree that in this situation she managed to get someone to put their job on the line, and if consequences were to arise Jane could blame everyone else while shunning the responsibility.

When Christmas came around we adopted the same plan as the year before.

"How can you justify unsupervised contact at Christmas but not at other times during the year?" Tanya later questioned.

"It's a one-off special occasion," I reasoned. "Should David suffer from it then there will be plenty of time to address the problem, as the other sessions are supervised."

The professionals, including Tanya, endorsed my argument.

Tanya called me and dropped by the house a number of times, and she would pass on messages from Adam Davies, David's solicitor, that Judge Renhold would insist on seeing progress each time we sat in court, which by now was every few months. I presented the same question each time I was told this: "What has changed since David was taken into care?" I knew nothing had changed, and situations such as that with Barbara trying to get involved at Jane's insistence did not convince me otherwise.

The only answer anyone ever presented was that David was growing older and learning how to understand his mother's behaviour. My response was always that more time was needed; for David to truly learn how to handle Jane's behaviour, he needed time away from it to grow and develop. All the time he was left unsupervised with Jane it was like she turned his developmental clock back.

It frustrated me that in spite of the statement from the psychologist that Jane was unlikely to accept responsibility and see a need to change, the legal process was pressuring us into moving forward with contact. Every time David spoke with Jane on the phone we could see the power she had over him, and we requested that other people witness his demeanour during a phone call to his mother so they could understand that his progress since coming to live with us was still extremely fragile. This was always acknowledged in the same way: a nod of heads with gritted teeth. It was to demonstrate an understanding that what we said was true, but that it didn't change the fact we needed to move forward.

By this point, David was doing well and he was seeing Jane every three weeks for dinner supervised by Dana. They were proving to be positive experiences for him, and he was also seeing his grandmother every week or fortnight. He would sometimes return from his grandmother's with some attitude, but this was quickly corrected.

I was notified of another final hearing date for May 2012 for the line to be drawn under David's case.

Chapter 23

The purchase of the new home was completed early in 2012, although we delayed moving in until Easter so we could decorate and modernise without having to live there while it was happening. Part of the agreement we had reached on holiday was that we would move house and get a dog; with the house now sorted, David regularly asked about when we could begin a search for a canine friend.

"We can start looking now if you like," Annie told him.

David readily agreed, and the two of them searched the Internet for what would become our latest family member. It didn't take long; within a week we were visiting a kennel just a few miles outside of town. The woman who owned it was instantly likeable, radiating confidence and love for animals, which instilled confidence in me that the animals were well looked after.

One of the dogs she had was a three-year-old male tri-colour border collie. He was there because the previous owner wanted him to be put to sleep as he could no longer keep him, but thankfully the vet had refused and sent it to the Dog's Trust instead.

We walked into a grooming-area-cum-kennel-style office and waited while the owner retrieved the dog for us. As soon as she opened the door he bounded into the room, tail wagging furiously and his big brown eyes full of affection and energy. He scanned the room, not knowing where to look or who to go to first, before nuzzling everyone quickly to say hello. When he reached David, it seemed both of them recognised a new best friend in the other. David began talking to the dog and in response the collie pricked his ears up and tilted his head as though trying to comprehend what David was saying.

We all knew straight away that this one was going to be living with us. His name was Patch and we would collect him at a later date when the relevant paperwork had been completed.

The day before the second final hearing in May the aptly named "court bundle" arrived, containing the documents being presented to the court from the other parties. Upon opening it, Annie and I were amazed to find a letter from Barbara, the sports club assistant, to the school headmaster stating that I had threatened her. I looked at the date of the letter and noticed it was two days after I had phoned the school, requesting that they speak with Barbara in regard to her staying out of David's case. The letter was several months old and I had never heard anything after phoning the school, when they had assured me the matter would be addressed. Although pleased that no action had been taken after the letter, I was disappointed that we hadn't been informed the school had received it, and it was extremely frustrating to see yet more false allegations being presented to the court.

The hearing was in the city again and so we started the familiar routine of arranging for David to stay at school if necessary and then fighting through commuter traffic. Lacking legal representation, Annie and I went straight to the court building where we met Tanya and Adam to discuss a joint proposal for contact. When we got into our private room they explained they were aware of our statement and also had instructions from Karen to insist on supervised contact until David turned sixteen, as well as an order under Section 91 (14) of the Children Act 1989 to ensure proceedings could not go back to court until two years had passed. I then raised the issue of Barbara's letter to the school.

"It is clearly her attempt to get herself out a hole that she dug for herself," Adam said dismissively. "However, the school *should* have told you about it and you have every right to an apology, especially considering the way you found out about it and how it was intended to be used against you." This was comforting, but Adam then caused us some distress: "Now, you may want to consider negotiating the demands of Jane's legal team because they will no doubt contest and if we fail to come to an amicable arrangement then Judge Renhold will simply make an order that may not be in our favour."

Annie and I had been concerned after Barbara's letter, and our confidence was now shaken further. We had made sure that everyone knew all along what Karen was advising, and she had commanded respect throughout the proceedings because she was the one professional who had recognised and raised concerns over David's abuse. But now, having believed that everyone was on-board and confident with Karen's recommendations, we were faced with being put on the spot in court and expected to negotiate a compromise.

Annie was clearly distressed, "How? Why? What has changed? The system is stacked against us and favours an abuser. Perjury and falsehoods flourish without any consequence, and are then used against us."

Tanya and Adam both nodded their heads to what Annie was saying. She continued "What if the role was reversed, would Tom be given such consideration? What is it about this system that demeans the role of a father and so reveres that of the mother?"

"I agree entirely," Adam responded, "but if the decision goes before the judge then there's a strong possibility he could rule otherwise."

We were where I had been years before on numerous occasions, and hindsight has once again shown me my error, as I realise now that we would have benefited from legal representation. Given that Adam wanted what was best for David as much as Annie and I did, we had felt he was all that was necessary.

Annie was deeply upset by now; we were both concerned for David and needed to restrict how much Jane could interfere in his development and our home life.

As I was mulling things over, someone rapped on the door and in walked the barrister that had supported Jane at the so-called "final hearing" sixteen months prior. He was a tall, slim man, in his late fifties with a mouthful of teeth that would seem at home on a Grand National winner. With overpowering theatrical exuberance, he introduced himself, to Tanya and Annie first, then Adam and myself.

With the pleasantries over, he addressed us in a tone of voice of aristocratic command: "I have taken instructions from my client, who wishes to have unsupervised overnight weekend contact with her son, together with two annual holidays."

Annie later confirmed her stomach hit the floor just as mine did, but we didn't have much time to acknowledge it because the barrister kept going.

"I have read the reports together with all the previous history of this case and the present statements from all the professionals involved, and consequently I have told my client that overnight contact will not be an option," he said, removing a two-tonne weight from my mind.

I understood this to be a clever tactic to place a stake in the ground from where we would negotiate, and making a statement followed by a counter-statement would lull us into willingly cooperating. He had essentially done the Good Cop, Bad Cop routine as a solo performance. He then reiterated what Adam had said before about needing to reach an agreement.

"I am of the belief that Jane will not adhere to any agreement made today," I explained. "Just hours after our last hearing I received a phone call from her asking to change the conditions."

The barrister looked me in the eye and said, "Jane will have to make sure she does as she is told this time. I will make that absolutely clear to her."

With that, we all agreed to move to the upstairs cafeteria so we could continue discussing things over coffee.

During the following three hours, Jane occupied one table with her usual brief and the barrister I had just spoken to, while Tanya, Adam, Annie and I occupied tables across the room. Between us were numerous other parties engaging in legal settlements.

The time it took to move to the cafeteria and queue for lukewarm drinks gave Annie and I time to exchange our thoughts on the contact proposal. It stood to reason that David would be highly likely to seek contact with Jane long before he turned sixteen, and even that would only happen on the chance that we could secure a ruling on supervised contact until he turned sixteen and not risk Judge Renhold ordering something we considered unsuitable. Jane lived just a few hundred metres away from David's school, which made policing an order for supervised contact extremely unrealistic. We therefore decided that we would have no choice but to compromise, but also to hold our ground until we got an idea of Jane's barrister's proposal, and go from there. We had made our position known, he then made Jane's wishes clear but dismissed them, so we decided not to change our stance before hearing their revised proposal.

Adam, Tanya, Annie and I discussed the possibilities.

"We need as much time as possible before David has unsupervised contact with Jane," I said to Adam.

"Yes, I understand fully and I will do everything I can to effect the best possible plan," he replied.

What really compounded our frustration was that we did not want to stop David seeing Jane. In fact, we would have loved to make a schedule around Jane's original request where David could spend every other weekend with his mother. All that was needed for that to happen was Jane to acknowledge her mistakes, take responsibility for them and demonstrate a willingness and ability to change. Sadly, after eleven years of repeating the same behaviour we knew that David's best interests meant digging our heels in and resisting anything that would be detrimental to him.

Jane's barrister wandered over to our table several times to discuss different scenarios. Several times Adam tried to speak and the barrister barked back, dismissing him. Adam took it in his stride but it was strange for me to see him not holding the reins.

Annie and I sat back listening, but offered no ground to negotiate – we decided it was best for them to fight it out because we would still have to be consulted before going in front of the judge. After more than two hours of to-and-fro debates, finally a plan emerged that we could present to Judge Renhold. Then Adam suggested that we needed the school to be fully aware of why David had been ordered into care in the first place, so with the agreement of Annie and I, he insisted the judge's ruling that ordered David into care should be released to the school, and used the letter from Barbara as proof that the school needed to be better informed of what had occurred in David's life. Barbara's bigoted corres-pondence had spurred us to rethink negotiating, but it had actually backfired and worked against her. Annie and I then suggested to Adam that, in addition to the school receiving the letter, we should send copies of the ruling to the after school sports club.

"That is highly unlikely to be agreed," Adam informed us. "The club is not entirely supervised by professionals, and so the chances are such a ruling will be dismissed."

The plan that we would use to compromise was that Dana and Jeff would supervise contact three hours once every three weeks. If everything was progressing smoothly after three months then David would start unsupervised contact for dinner with Jane at her home for two hours a week. No one other than Jane, her mother or Graham would be present without us being informed in writing in advance, and with us agreeing to it. If the situation was still progressing without problems after six months, contact would extend to four hours unsupervised at the weekend, and a further three months later would mean a day of contact occurring for one day every other weekend, and a two-hour dinner visit every other week. There were, however, to be no overnight visits. These conditions were neatly written down and photocopies were made before we entered court.

There wasn't much enthusiasm as we entered the courtroom – neither party was happy with the compromise, but that's the nature of compromise.

After Judge Renhold had entered and was seated, Jane's barrister began a condescending preamble that detailed what we had agreed. Adam stood next and confirmed that the legal guardian supported the agreement. The judge then looked to me for my explanation of the understanding that had been reached.

I stood. "Firstly sir, may I apologise in advance for not being as articulate as either of my predecessors," I started.

Judge Renhold smiled at me, assuring me that I was doing fine.

I then gave an outline of facts, stating how Annie and I had jumped through every hoop regardless of how high they had been raised, as well as adhering to every instruction that had ever been asked of us. "We have, at all times, acted in the best interest of David and at all times made decisions only after full and in-depth consultations with all of the involved professionals. I would also like to point out that we have ensured David continued to see his maternal grandmother, and reassured him repeatedly that his mother loves him and none of what has transpired is his fault. I have always maintained that David should enjoy a full and proper relationship with his entire family, including his mother.

David is progressing very well, but his understanding of what has happened to him is dangerously thin, so it will not take much for any of that progress to be reverted. Karen Woodall, from the Centre for Separated Families, advised us to insist on supervised contact only and for a 91 (14) order, because of the need for David to have further time to develop. We also need to monitor progress closely."

The mannerisms I saw from the judge made me believe him to be in agreement with what I had said, and for a few moments I started to doubt succumbing to the pressure of compromising away from Karen's instructions. Here I was, in court with a judge who appeared to respect my opinions and endeavours to protect my son, and I could imagine him agreeing to uphold the original insistence of Karen for supervised contact until David turned sixteen. Nonetheless, the compromise had been reached so I reassured myself that we would be able to manage the circumstances.

"I share your concerns, Mr Moore, and see these proposals as acceptable. What financial agreement have you made with Dana and Jeff?" Judge Renhold asked.

"Both Dana and Jeff are happy to be active in David's life and there is no remuneration beyond their meals being paid for."

Judge Renhold commended Dana and Jeff, and requested Adam and Tanya to extend to them the court's thanks. He then stated there was a possibility of a 91 (14) order being attached to the ruling.

"Sir, there is insufficient grounds for such an order," Jane's barrister contested.

"This child is not thirteen years of age, and yet eleven years of his life have been embroiled in Family Court,"

Judge Renhold countered and glanced at me. "Mr Moore must be exhausted with this process and David himself is due some respite. The eleven years justify the 91 (14) order so that a return to court will not be possible for two years. I further approve that the previous ruling for David to be taken into care shall be released to the school, however Mr Moore I must decline your request for the same to be sent to the sport club, on the grounds that it is not operated fully by professionals."

When all had been formalised, the barrister presented the judge with the Legal Aid paperwork. Somewhere in the back of my mind I heard the echo of the first CAFCASS officer involved, eleven years earlier: "Her Legal Aid will run out soon."

When we returned home I was upbeat in delivering information about contact to David, and he took the detail of the plan positively. Tanya and Adam visited a few days later to talk to David about the ruling and reassure him one more time that none of these events were his fault. They also left him a copy of the court order and Adam told David that he could call him if he was ever worried.

Earlier that day we collected our new canine friend from the Dog's Trust and David had shown him to Tanya and Adam, before walking them up to the top of the garden to show them his beehive.

When they went to leave, out of earshot of David Adam turned to Tanya. "Things have turned out very fortunately for David . . . and the dog."

Fortunate as it may have been, Patch the dog was restless on his first night and did not settle quietly. This meant Annie and I not having a good night's rest either, as we were up every hour to try to get him to stop barking or howling.

In the morning, with bleary eyes we entered a messy utility room and a nervous Patch greeting us. Despite the mess, we made a fuss of him and showed him a lot of affection so he knew he was safe and loved in his new home.

As we settled him down for the second night, David was very attentive to the dog. We all ensured that Patch was in his bed and closed the door expecting to be disturbed during the night again – but we couldn't have been more wrong. When we woke in the morning and went into the utility room, Patch was still in his bed and there was no mess to clean up. David and I took him into the garden and I expressed how good it was that the dog had settled so well the second night.

David called Patch, and the dog responded immediately with a bounce and wagging tail. David stroked him, threw the ball and smiled. "Dad, he was bound to be upset the first night; he will have been very confused. But now he knows we all care about him and he's safe, he's worked it out and he'll be fine."

Epilogue

Six months after the second final hearing, and about thirty months after David was taken into care, I am pleased to write this chapter with the report that progress is going to plan. David is currently seeing his mother unsupervised each weekend for four hours, plus two hours one evening a week for dinner. We are looking forward to progressing to one full day every other weekend.

Being removed from his mother has had a profound positive effect on David – friends, family and professionals have all independently told us that he is a "different child". He is demonstrating responsibility too: Patch and David are the best of friends, and the bees are well established in their hive at the top of the garden. David will be turning fourteen soon and he is showing the typical teenage independence by arranging his own schedule in which to see his friends. We are cautiously optimistic for the future.

The three of us try to meet with Dana and Jeff for dinner once a month, and James remains in contact, still occasionally stopping by for tea, chocolate cake and updates on David.

Life remains busy, especially with Emily and Paul scheduled to wed in New Zealand, so that is a trip we are planning. Annie remains as supportive as ever and we are enjoying the new house as a family. Any sailing plans we make now are scheduled around the school holidays, and David is always included. With all the court battles hopefully behind us, I have built a strong relationship with my son and while I provide him a home and love, he enriches my life. I can say, for the first time in over a decade, that life is good.

I haven't come away from the eleven-year tug-of-war without any opinions on how the system should change, though. Having been put through the mill of it, it is my firm belief that the Family Law process needs to be dramatically restructured, but until that happens there are simple suggestions to improve the current practice.

When CAFCASS is made aware of a child and creates a record of it, that record should be kept until the child reaches adolescence, rather than being destroyed after a couple of years. It is logical that if multiple trips to court have been necessary when the child is just an infant, then it's likely future problems will arise.

Only one judge should preside over the case. I believe that if there had been one overseeing judge from the first day, things would have been better in our case. Judge Renhold took it upon himself to champion the case after I insulted the court, and while I am grateful that he did, the fact is I should not have had to express my contempt of court for a judge to take my assertions seriously.

In this age of technology, it should have been easy for the professionals involved in the meeting to decide whether David should be put on the Child Protection register – school, Social Services, CAFCASS, the police and the family doctor – should have access to share notes and information. This would quicken the pace and flag areas of concern. It would also work to avoid any disputes or delays based in ignorance.

Legal Aid needs to be drastically altered. In our court case, Legal Aid, and by default the public's taxes, was being successfully used to cause further abuse to my son.

I do not advocate further involvement of the existing nanny state into our personal lives. In order to minimise the risk of children being used as weapons in parental disputes, and subject to there being no evidence of cause for concern, the Family Court process should have a default basic contact schedule for an estranged parent following no more than two court appearances. Further progress can be made thereafter if necessary.

Perjury and false accounts should be punished severely rather than let go as they were in our case. If the process continues to fail then both parents (and grandparents if they are involved) should attend compulsory parenting classes, such as those offered by the Centre for Separated Families. It is shameful that speeding drivers must attend classes on speed awareness, but our role as parents receives less consideration.

Any parent that has been found guilty of abusing their child, to the point that the child has been removed from their care, should be named on a national database and directed to undergo classes to improve the situation. As things stand, though, there are no such consequences, and Jane was simply able to refuse to attend parenting classes or any other help available to her.

There are several facts that should be noted, because David's life would have turned out very differently otherwise. If I had been employed full-time, rather than self-employed and able to schedule my work as necessary, then I would either have been unable to attend court, or unable to pay for the legal bills. Either way, the court cases would probably not have occurred. My self-employment meant that on many occasions I was working at three o'clock in the morning so that I could be free for an afternoon in court.

Had Annie and I not been together then I doubt any single working man could have coped or even received the same acceptance of being able to manage from Social Services. Furthermore, if we had lived in the city rather than a small town, it is likely that Social Services would not have held the resources to act as efficiently as they eventually did.

Perhaps what is most concerning is that if I had not taken it upon myself to make, and keep, notes on every time David was ill or a contact session was cancelled, there would have been nothing to show the pattern and therefore nothing to present to a professional for them to see something was amiss. The chances are that David would have been abused for many more years had I not made those notes.

The most powerful event, though, was meeting Karen Woodall, whose experience and wisdom pushed me to pursue what was right for my son. Karen gave me the information and tools necessary to push forward in court, and got involved by writing an excellent report that demonstrated to everyone exactly what was going on.

I first began writing this story simply as notes, a few lines here and there to work out my frustration. Slowly, cataloguing the events became an escape. Eventually I began to think I would be estranged from David forever so I wrote the story down because I thought it would be valuable to him later in life, so he could understand what we had all been through. When I met Karen though, I realised it was a turning point and that perhaps other people could benefit from my experiences – whether that be drawing effective information to help them or just a way of not feeling alone, in the same way I had joined a forum for fathers. Aside from all that though, I felt it was necessary to highlight the incompetence, failures and hypocrisy of the legal process, not to mention a tremendous misplacement of public money. I would like David's story to help enact some changes in the Family Law process so other families will not have to endure what we did – and a sizeable sum of money could be saved from the taxpayers' purse too.

My story is the same as that of many other estranged parents and frightened children; Parental Alienation, although it may not be the worst breach of human rights in the world, it is avoidable through legislation and education. It begs the question, "Which of our politicians will champion the issue?"